HONKY

stories
by
benjamin drevlow

COWBOY JAMBOREE PRESS
good grit lit

Copyright © 2024 by Benjamin Drevlow

All rights reserved. No part of this book may be reproduced or used in any manner without written permission of the copyright owner except for the use of quotations in a book review. For more information, address: cowboyjamboree@gmail.com

First Edition
ISBN: 9798335260534

Unless otherwise indicated, all the names, characters, businesses, places, events, and incidents in this book are either the product of the author's imagination or used in a creative manner. No harm is intended to persons, living or dead.

Cover Design: Benjamin Drevlow & Christopher Smith
Interior Design: Adam Van Winkle

Cowboy Jamboree Press
good grit lit
www.cowboyjamboreemagazine.com/books

For Boykin, Ida, Kelly, Tyra, Q, TC, Kevin, et al.

Praise for HONKY

The late, great Lewis Nordan assured our geographies made us, and I have a feeling Benjamin Drevlow would agree. The risky endeavors connecting the stories of *Honky* chart geographies from Northernass Wisconsin and the longings of a white boy with heroes like Air Jordan, Tupac, and Biggie to Southernass Georgia with that grown up boy trying to do right in a world he struggles to comprehend. Hot damn, Drevlow is on to something genuine, with prose so pure I guarantee you'll fly through these pages so you can start all over again.

> – Tom Williams, author of *Among the Wild Mulattos and Other Stories*

Like all vital work, *Honky* raises questions: about the nature of white American masculinity, about the choices we make for or against our upbringings. Drevlow's work alternates between the crude, the touching, and the hilarious. If it were up to me, I'd name Drevlow the poet laureate of Northernass Wisconsin.

> – Leland Cheuk, author of *No Good Very Bad Asian*

In his new collection of linked short stories, Benjamin Drevlow creates a persona, a character: a bumbling white guy named Ben Drevlow who is over-eager to be accepted by the Black people in his life—on the basketball court, at work, in his neighborhood—but who also has an uncanny knack for faux pas that often gets in the way. The Ben Drevlow of *Honky* is a welcome counter to the aggrieved white guy trope we've had to suffer through for the last decade, actually for basically forever. He seeks acceptance, belonging, connection, and when he doesn't always get what he wants he doesn't turn to anger. He has the awareness to recognize not everything is about himself. He's always trying to be a good person, and always aware that he's not always as good a person as he wants to be, but he never stops trying, and that's the thing that makes him good, because the world is full of people who do stop trying. These stories are funny, absurd, heart-wrenching, sometimes cringe-worthy, but they're also real and filled with respect and introspection. Benjamin Drevlow writes his heart out.

> – Alan Good, Malarkey Books and author of *The Sun Still Shines on a Dog's Ass*.

Benjamin Drevlow writes, "White guilt can be a powerful motivating factor in proving you're not racist like your neighbors." The moment encapsulates a lot of what *Honky* is about when it comes to well-meaning white people, performative anti-racist sentiments, and the complexities of navigating interpersonal relationships. More than an allegory or politicized rant, this collection is unapologetically blunt in using tools like basketball and hip-hop to give the reader much more food for thought than the narrator himself can digest. *Honky* is not for the faint of heart but it is a book that should go on the reading list of anyone interested in developing empathy, celebrating grit, and getting in a few good laughs along the way.

    – Michael Chin, author of *This Year's Ghost* and *My Grandfather's an Immigrant, and So Is Yours*

Honky is a tour de force. It is at once investigative and deeply personal. Often asking the hard questions directed/targeted at oneself, one's whiteness, at Drevlow's history and/or coming-of-age. In the same way Crew's *A Childhood* turned the pen inwards, so does Drevlow's *Honky*. Self-exploration is a difficult task and racial tension a hard subject, especially in a climate like today. *Honky* is visceral and gripping and above all nuanced—Drevlow should be applauded for striking that balance.

    – Sacha Bissonnette, *Wigleaf Top Fifty*

The world needs wannabes.

– The Offspring, Pretty Fly (For a White Guy)

PART I. NORTHERNASS WISCONSIN

Dad: Act I	12
Dad: Act II	14
Ray: Act I	23
Ray: Act II	24
Tyra Banks	25
Ida Samuels-Buffalo	27
The Fighting Little People	29
Boykin	32
KellyKellyKelly	39
Mr. Good Samaritan	47
Joy	49
Q	53
Shonda	62
TC	70
Deputy Scotty	92

PART II. SOUTHERNASS GEORGIA

Clem & Mel & Mikey   106

Nurse Bernie   124

Roadrage Lady   130

Honey Baby Darlin Sweetie Pie 134

Harold & Reggie   139

Benjamin/Benjamin   150

[Name Redacted]   153

Barbie   155

Burger King Guy: Act I   157

Kevin   160

MJ   182

Burger King Guy: Act II   185

PART I.
NORTHERNASS
WISCONSIN

DAD: ACT I

I AM BORN IN A DOUBLEWIDE out near the barrens where they've cleared the small handful of trees to build my dad's house—he's not an architect or a construction worker. He is an electrical engineer and a farm kid who grew up milking cows and harvesting beets. He's designed and built the house himself, though I'm sure he's had help, but I am too young to remember.

I am not born in a doublewide, I am born in the woods, a shack, the log house my dad built for my brothers, a tree fort, the stream that runs through our ravine to the pond the cows drink on their way to the barn.

I am not born in the woods, I am born in a hospital 20 minutes away but spend my first year in a double-wide waiting for my dad to build his house, I'm sure my brothers, four and seven, do their fair share of work as well. As my mother tells it me anyway.

My dad doesn't tell stories.

I cry and cry. I am colicky. I am a crybaby. I am a mama's boy. From the time I am born the baby of three brothers to today at 45 years young. I may cry right now as I remember this as I write it.

Ten years later my oldest brother will shoot himself in his bedroom which is originally my room—designed to be my room with cartoonish farm wallpaper full of cows and horses and tractors and barns. My brother never will never ask to take it down. He will just move in and I will be moved out, then moved in with my other brother down the hall, my closet sharing my brother's bedside where he will one day he shoot himself. Blowing his brains out across so much cartoon agriculture.

Three years later I will accidentally burn my dad's house down—two space heaters in the back of my closet to keep warm while I learn to masturbate. The only room that will be left untouched by the fire, my brother's, which originally is supposed to be mine—the farming wallpaper having been scrubbed of all that blood, having now turned yellow with soot, but still there, still up.

I am born my dad's son, my mother's substitute daughter, my brother's brother.

I have nothing but stories to tell you, some of them true, the stories you'll never hear from anybody but me.

DAD: ACT II

I'M 13 YEARS OLD.
I'm working on my ball handling down by the shop and listening to O.P.P. by Naughty by Nature—unaware that my dad is inside the shop fixing a tractor.

I realize that he's been listening to my O.P.P. when he walks out, walks over to my boom box, takes out the tape, and snaps it in my face.

We don't need this crap, he says.

He says my name: Ben, we don't need this crap.

I put my head down and mumble sorry, won't happen again.

He goes back to fixing the tractor.

My eyes start to well up as I look at the snapped tape near my feet, the unspooled thread. I start mumbling and crying a little and go back to working on my killer crossover like: *Yeah, I'm tough real tough. I'm not gonna cry because my daddy snapped my favorite Naughty by Nature tape.*

Stupid crap, I keep whispering under my breath as tears stream down and I break imaginary people's ankles. *Stupid crap. It's not stupid crap.*

I'm listening to my O.P.P. again later that night when my mom comes down and taps me on the headphones. She wants to talk.

She says my name. She says, Ben, can we talk?

I'm concerned that she might have spoken to my dad about OPP and now that she has heard the muffled lyrics through my headphones, she is about to give me the sex talk.

My mother teaches Home Ec. at my school, which for some reason also means she teaches middle school sex ed. I am not in seventh grade yet and have yet to be traumatized by my mother teaching me sex ed in middle school.

Right now I'm focusing on the fact that my mother giving me the sex talk about OPP is going to be traumatizing enough on its own.

My mother does not snap OPP in my face. She picks up the walkman and shows it to me: Do you like the lyrics or the sound of the music?

I say the sound of the music. (Which is a lie. I'm a connoisseur of both).

You know, she says, that's what I thought.

Then she hands me back my walkman and says, Well, let's just try to keep this between you and me. You know how your dad is.

My dad is the son of a Lutheran minister. He has gone to church pretty much every Sunday of his entire life, sung in the choir, collected offering, read the selected bible verses of the day out loud, and volunteered as the assistant minister once a month.

Outside church, my dad isn't one of those churchy people who want to make a big deal about it for everyone to see. We pray for lunch and dinner but he's not all like *Thank the Lord, Praise be, Bless your heart, Lord Almighty, Save my Soul, Teach me the Path, Forgive me my sins, Father, Son, and Holy Ghost.*

On the other hand, he doesn't swear or use the Lord's name in vain or dirty talk.

He says things like *crap* and *criminy*, *sheesh* and *for Pete's sake*, and uff dah (as in *uff dah the heat is just the blazes today*).

I play basketball, shave my head, wear shorts off my ass and past my knees, and listen to songs about bitches, hoes, and OPP.

I don't go around calling women bitches or hoes or talking about OPP. I especially don't go throwing the n-word around.

But I've been known to throw out a *fuck you motherfuckin cocksuckin son of a bitch* from time to time.

But usually at myself. Like when I'd miss a layup or dribble the ball off the shoe: *fuck you motherfuckin cocksuckin son of a bitch.*

I just like the music. And the lyrics. And how it makes me feel all tough and badass and not like the crybaby sensitive high-strung kid I am who cries every time his daddy yells at him.

I'm 16 when my dad snaps Tupac in my face.

I've forgotten my mixtape in my dad's work truck after having hauled my friends to a streetball tournament in town that weekend.

I can hear the quick clipped blast of music as I walk out to my mom's car to get a ride to school.

It's the one where Tupac calls out Biggie with disses like: *That's why I fucked yo bitch, you fat motherfucker.* And: *Fuck your bitch and the clique you claim.* And: *You claim to be a player but I fucked your wife.*

But my dad doesn't get to the chorus.

I try to act surprised when he walks over to me in my mother's car and snaps it in my face.

Through clenched teeth: *I… thought… I… said… we… don't… need… this… crap…?*

I put my head down and mumble sorry it won't happen again.

If… I… ever… hear… this… again… he says. He doesn't finish. Just stomps back to the truck and heads to work.

My mom watches it happen without saying anything and then gets in the car next to me: Oh you know your dad.

On the way to school, she says, Do you think you could try listening to more rap music that isn't so vulgar? Maybe the PG rap songs? I've heard they even have Christian rap songs?

My mom says, Well I just think we need to be a little more careful about leaving things in the car.

I say, But Ma, it's just that sometimes I get sad and depressed and frustrated and feeling down about myself and the rap songs help me vent everything out, you know, so I don't feel so bad about myself?

My mom says, Oh that's nice. And then she says: If only your dad had an outlet like that.

I'm 18 when my dad snaps DMX in my face.

His truck has broken down. It's in the shop for a week, and for some reason, he chooses me to drive him to work instead of my mother.

So I have to drive him to work in the Bronco II he has rebuilt for me for my 18th birthday.

The first morning I turn the key and immediately DMX starts growling, *N****** wanna try, n****** wanna lie / Then n****** wonder why, n****** wanna die.*

My dad doesn't say anything this time. He smashes like eight buttons until he finds the eject button. He shows me the DMX CD, snaps it in half, snaps it in quarters, unrolls the window and deposits the jagged little quarters out into the ditch.

A lot of kids, by the time they turn 18, they're not afraid to back-talk their dad. A lot of 18-year-olds might've said that's not fair! and Why'd you do that for? I'm 18 now. You can't do that to my stuff anymore.

It's a rite of passage: challenging the old man, showing you can stand up for yourself.

Then again, a lot of kids don't have dads like mine. Minister's kid. Having been born at the start of WWII. Six foot three, 220 pounds, former starting center for a state championship basketball team, DI college line-backer, swarthy German skin, middle name Adolph, having once cut off his finger and went back to baling hay the rest of the day until sunset.

I don't dare look him in the face. I don't want to show him the tears welling up in my eyes. The fear trembling in my fingers on the steering wheel. I don't want to be insolent, I don't want to be spineless. I am not ready to pass this rite of passage.

I say sorry and turn my head and try not to let him hear me sniffle.

We sit in silence for 25 minutes on the way to his work.

When we get there, he says, Be back by 5. Slams the door behind him.

I continue sitting in silence for the 25 minutes it takes me to drive back across town to my own school. Muttering to myself *stupid stupid dad stupid DMX stupid rap stupid stupid stupid*.

It's the same silent routine the rest of the week.

If you're looking for a story about a young man learning to stand up for himself, this is not your story.

If you're looking for a story about my dad trying to understand me and my musical interests more, this is not your story.

If you're looking for a story where my dad explains to me why rap is degrading to women and promotes violence and toxic masculinity and I internalize his message and only listen to Christian rock the rest of my life…

This is not your story.

I have never sworn in front of my dad. I have never back-talked my dad. I have never even looked my dad in the eyes for one of his lectures.

I have let my dad see and hear me cry in response to his lectures too many times for it not to be a source of embarrassment for both of us.

When I was little I loved GI Joes; I never enrolled in the military, never shot a gun in my life.

I loved WWF wrestling. I have never worn a wrestling singlet, never punched anybody in my life.

Before I was 13 years old, I had watched *Die Hard*, *Beverly Hills Cop*, and *Lethal Weapon*. I never joined the police force or blew up any buildings.

I watched *The Matrix* six times and never shot up my school.

My dad never beat me. Never called me a pussy or the f-word. Never told me I threw like a girl. Or to suck it up, buttercup and be a man.

These are just some of the sometimes-confusing facts about my relationship with my dad.

It's the Sunday before I graduate from high school, the church we go to—the church where my dad sings in the choir every week and volunteers to be assistant minister and take up the offering and read the bible verses—they are doing a special service celebrating me and the other graduating seniors.

There are 11 of us.

The service starts with one girl singing God Bless America with her mom playing organ and her dad playing guitar.

Then three students get together with two other students from their high school acapella group to do the song Spirit in the Sky rockapella style.

Two angsty Christian punks do an air guitar version of Jesus Freak by DC Talk.

I do not sing.

I have a dad who grew up in the church choir with seven siblings who sound like the Mormon Tabernacle Choir if the Mormon Tabernacle Choir was Lutheran and even more repressed.

I do not sing.

I do a spoken-word poem about how much I like basketball. I recite my *spoken-word poem* line by line from a wrinkly piece of notebook paper from the lectern without looking up or taking a breath.

My poem has nothing to do with God, but it does not have any *bitches, hoes,* or *n-words* in it. It has a couple vague references to a higher power and the lines: *When I'm feelin in the zone and my jumper is a flowin / everybody in the house be knowin / I'm about to throw it down, yo.*

I get about as many claps as the air guitar dudes. I do not look up to see the look on my dad's face. Nor do I look for the affirmation of my mom's face.

I sit back down and stare at my poem scribbled on my notebook and think *stupid spoken-word poem, stupid stupid poem, stupid rap stupid stupid basketball church stupid dad stupid Jesus stupid God stupid stupid.*

The final act is three guys dressed up like Eminem in white t-shirts and blond hair. They get up there and immediately urge the congregation to clap along: *Get your hands in the air and show Jesus just how much you care.*

They do Rapper's Delight by Sugar Hill Gang but with their own remixed Christian version.

It includes lyrics like *I said-a hip, hop, the hippie, the hippie / to the top of the cross—let Jesus be your rock.*

And: *Now what you hear is a test of faith: I'm a prayin on my knees. / It's me, my savior, and the Holy Ghost, we're gonna try to get you off your seat.*

And: *Skiddlee beebop a' we rock a faith that's true / And guess what, Christians: we love you Cause ya talk to the Lord with so much soul / Place your faith in God and walk his walk and you'll be saved when you're a thousand and one years old.*

The whole congregation is on their feet, clapping and rapping along by the end of it.

Including my dad.

On the car ride home, I sit on the end of the bench seat of my dad's truck with my mom in the middle. My mother turns to tell me how much she enjoyed my little poem. It had some really neat rhymes in it, she says. I knew all those years of listening to your rap songs would pay off.

My dad takes his eyes off the road for the first time in his life to make eye contact with me around my mother's head. He's smiling the biggest smile I've ever seen him smile.

He does not share my mother's sentiments. He does not mention anything about my spoken-word poem or if all those years of listening to my rap songs have paid off.

Now you wanna talk about some good rap music, he says. Hippity-hoppity let Jesus be your rock. Maybe if some of your rappers could rap like that..., well, I don't know. Then we'd have something.

I say, Yeah. Sorry. Totally.

My mom looks back at me and rolls her eyes. Shakes her head. Don't listen to your dad, she says and pats my thigh. Your poem was way more tight than their hippity-hop nonsense.

I don't know about that, my dad says. That was pretty catchy. He starts humming it to himself, mumbling the lyrics under this breath.

This is the last time I talk to my dad or mother about rap. I learn my lesson. I switch to MP3s.

I go away to college. I stop coming home as soon as I make the basketball team and find my people. Mostly they're a bunch of big black dudes from the streets of Chicago and Minneapolis and even some from NYC, dudes who appreciate my love for DMX and Pac and especially OPP. Guys who talk like they talk, about bitches and hoes and callin each other the n-word, *my n-word, yo n-word*.

And I make them all mixes and we talk about who are the true OGs, the Mount Rushmore OGs, and East Coast vs. West

Coast, Biggie vs. Pac, and even though they never call me their n-word, they still call me a word that rhymes with the n-word: it starts with *w*. Sometimes they even say, *yo, what up, my w-n-word.*

RAY: ACT I

MY BIG BROTHER RAY TEASES ME ruthlessly for wetting the bed.

At one point he convinces me that I'm going to wet the bed on the electric heating pad and electrocute myself and burn down the whole house in the process.

I show him.

I may wet the bed until I'm 13 but I don't electrocute myself.

I may accidentally burn down the house when I am 14 and I fall asleep after masturbating to the *Sports Illustrated Swimsuit Edition* and forget to turn the space heaters off before I leave for school.

But joke's on Ray.

He's already been dead two years by the time I burn the house down.

I think about this a lot at night when it's cold and I want to turn the heat on.

Or when I wake up and am deciding whether or not I can get back to sleep without peeing.

Or when I feel guilty about masturbating.

Or when I think about what a sick puppy my brother was before he killed himself.

Or when I think about karma.

Or killing myself.

RAY: ACT II

THE DAY BEFORE HE TURNS 18, Ray commits three acts of kindness:
    1. He picks up his senior photos for Mom.
    2. He fixes the tractor for Dad.
    3. He puts up a new basketball hoop for me.[1]

---

[1] If he had convinced himself that this would soften the emotional blow of the whole *blowing-your-brains-out-in-the-next-room* trauma, I assure you it did not.

TYRA BANKS

I AM 14 WHEN I BURN THE HOUSE DOWN masturbating in the closet.

This isn't entirely true but isn't not entirely true either.

It's early November in Northernass Wisconsin.

As the locals say: it's colder than a witch's titty.

And we have a wood furnace.

Which might work better if my dad didn't believe so heartily in energy conservation.

I've stolen two space heaters from our barn.

From lambing season.

Instead of using them to keep newborn lambs from freezing, I use them to keep myself and myself warm.

It's the issue of *Sports Illustrated* with Tyra Banks on the cover.

I exhaust myself quickly.

My room has the best, softest carpet.

I fall asleep (because I've exhausted myself).

I forget to set my alarm.

The next morning my mother storms in to ask why I'm not up yet for school.

I hop to and such and such.

I bumble and fumble around the way they do in movies.

But I manage to get my pants on and get to school on time.

I forget the heaters.

Forget the foldout of Tyra lying there next to the heaters.

I get called to the office in sixth-hour study hall.

Over the loudspeaker, they tell me that my sheep have gotten out and are eating the neighbor's flower garden.

Which is a lie.

My house is on fire.

More accurately:

I've set my house on fire masturbating.

The fire starts on my side of the house.

I cry and cry and I'm 16 and it's ugly but I keep crying to my mom that it was all my fault.

I tell her about the space heaters. I tell her about reading *Sports Illustrated*.

I don't tell her about Tyra's boobs.

My mother tries to tell me it isn't my fault.

It was the shitty wood furnace.

I don't believe her and I still don't believe her.

She never shows me any official report.

And anyway, my mom would never have it in her to blame me for burning the house down with my careless masturbating.

And now she's dead.

If there's a heaven, and if that heaven is the heaven they show on TV, she's up there somewhere with a big, beautiful house.

Knowing the truth about the Tyra's boobs.

RIP Mom.

RIP house.

RIP Tyra Banks's big boobs.

IDA SAMUELS-BUFFALO

IT'S THE YEAR the guys from my high school basketball team all watch *School Ties*, which is like a big launching pad for the careers of Matt Damon, Ben Affleck, Cole Hauser, Chris O'Donnell, and Brendan Frazier, but my friends' main take away from it is how funny it is to call things *Jewish*.

I'm not gonna pretend that I was up there lecturing on the history of the Holocaust.

We live in Northernass Wisconsin so there are no actual Jewish people within 100 miles.

Except for this one girl Ida Samuels-Buffalo who is half-Jewish, half-Native American whose mother died giving birth to her, her dad taking off not long after, leaving her to grow up with her Native American grandparents, learning traditions, not the least of which, being basketball, or rez ball as they call it (us too) the starting point guard for our biggest rival the Red Cliff Indians.

Them being from an actual rez with actual Native Americans, they can get away with calling themselves Indians.

Before *School Ties*, one of those redneck friends Timmy Knutson had dated her for a couple months before she dumped him, presumably because he is redneck racist misogynist asshole who only wanted her for her big tits and for how good she was at handling big balls. (His joke, not mine).

For weeks afterward, it's goddamn *b*-word this and goddamn *b*-word that. And sometimes the *c*-word and the *d*-word. Even though based on his stories she is anything but a *d*-word.

Then like I say we watch *School Ties* and suddenly it's *J*-word this and *J*-word that and *J*-word everything.

Which could've even gotten worse if he'd known that I've started dating Ida behind his back, me, myself, being a connoisseur of girls' basketball and the art ball handling.

Of course it's up in the barrens of Northernass Wisconsin with maybe 1500 people within an hour radius, 60 kids in our class, 30 kids in Ida's class, so obviously Timmy finds out eventually and turns his focus on me with *k*-word lover and *J*-word fucker.

Which is when, depending on your perspective, I stop being friends with him for being an antisemitic prick or he stops being friends with me for being a backstabbing *J*-word fucker.

It's the same with the rest of my redneck teammates—the difference of perspectives.

I'd like to think it's because I'm not at heart a redneck bigot, but I wouldn't be completely honest if I didn't mention the appeal of Ida's tits and ball handling abilities, and despite what Timmy would tell you, her quite enthusiastic and generous blowjobs.

Biggest of all, her wanting to have sex with me.

On top of her being a half-Jewish, half-Native American girl in Northernass Wisconsin—about as exotic a girl as you could find up there.

Though we never *do it* do it.

I'd like to tell you that it is because I am too much of a gentleman.

When actually it is because I'm not a good enough ball handler for her.

I never could master the two-step crossover between the legs and behind the back.

And she could never accept anything less than excellence as a baller.

THE FIGHTING LITTLE PEOPLE

EVERY YEAR MY HIGH SCHOOL basketball team plays two different teams named the Midgets.

This means that twice a year we come out onto the court through a run-thru that says *Stomp the Midgets*.

We are the Castle Guards.

The rest of the run-thru is a crude drawing from an artistic cheerleader depicting a knight stomping the little head of a little person.

They aren't the Fighting Little People, though.

They're the Butternut Midgets.

And the Hurley Midgets.

Both their actual mascots are knockoffs of the Notre Dame Fighting Irish mascot.

This being Northernass Wisconsin all the schools dot the shores of Lake Superior.

A state represented by the Green Bay [Meat] Packers, the Milwaukee [Beer] Brewers, and the Milwaukee [Male Deer We'd Like to Shoot, Skin, Gut, and Cook Up Come Hunting Season] Bucks.

The Drummond Lumberjacks (or Lumberjills for the girls).

The Ashland Ore Dockers (or Dockerettes)

The Mellen Granite Diggers (alas no Diggerettes or Diggeresses)

We have the Bayfield Trollers (again, no Trollerettes or Trolleresses)

There are two reservations of Chippewa on either side of us.

It is both racist and racist that none of the teams in the Indian Head Athletic Conference are named the Fighting Indians or the Mighty Chippewa.

It is not beyond the realm of racist possibilities that we could've run through a run-thru stenciled with *Scalp the*

Fighting Indians or *Offer the Mighty Chippewa False Promises of Not Running Them Off Their Native Lands.*

The story of the Hurley Midgets is that Hurley was originally founded as mining town for a bunch of kids of Italian immigrants who'd come to make a living crawling into small holes and caves.

In a football game 80 years ago, an opposing team announcer says derisively, Look like a buncha midgets out there runnin around.

This is what we do in Northernass Wisconsin.

We don't name our team the Mighty Miners.

We name our team the Fighting Midgets.

As a big fuck you to everyone who makes fun of us.

And a big fuck you to everyone who might be a little person and be offended by being called a midget.

These are my people.

Why were we the Castle Guards with a knight as our mascot and not the Knights with a knight as our mascot?

Once upon a time, people used to say that our original school building looked like a castle.

I've seen photos.

It looked a lot more like another kind of building with guard towers.

Imagine the potential for pep rallies:

Let's shiv the Prison Guards!

Let's bribe the Correction Officers!

Being proud of who we really are and not who we'd like to be only goes so far.

In 2019, Hurley High School votes to change their mascot from Mighty Midgets to the North Stars.

Which is a step in the right direction, but still:

That's a little like changing the Mighty Miners to the Fighting Constellations.

Let's Cloud Over the North Stars?

Let's Outshine the North Stars with Light Pollution?

Butternut has not even brought it to a vote.

Not even when the obvious alternative is right there for the taking:

Let's Go Squish the Squash!

They have also not won the conference in any sport in my lifetime.

Which maybe is the real tragedy of politically incorrect cultural appropriation:

It's one thing to be calling yourself the Midgets when you're winning.

It's a whole other thing to call yourself the Midgets when you're getting stomped, trampled, squished, squashed, run over, steamrolled, flattened, and tossed out with the trash every year.

Just imagine what it's like to be a little person reading those headlines:

Midgets lose again.
Midgets lose again.
Midgets lose again.

BOYKIN

BOYKIN'S THE ONLY BLACK KID I know growing up. His family the only black family in our redneck boony school of 150 students in Northernass Wisconsin.

Boykin's out on the basketball court shooting hoops at recess, steals the ball from me and won't give it back and when I try to grab it from him, he says, Back up, whiteboy and holds up his fist and tells me the story of his sister, in seventh grade, beating Devon Trubiczek over the head with a metal baseball bat and putting him in the hospital.

All because he'd called her the n-word.

And that's my sis, he says.

This is the first time I think about black versus white and Boykin being black versus me being white and the whole school being white except for Boykin and his sister Melody and his other older sister Crystal who weighs 300 pounds and who will eat me if I ever fuck with her or him or any of them in their family.

Or ever even consider thinking about them and the n-word in the same sentence.

This is what Boykin's told me. He's only sometimes joking.

My mother, who teaches Home Ec and has Crystal in class, says, Oh for pete's sake she's not that big and she's very very nice and she's always talking about how it's so nice that you and Matthew play basketball together because he doesn't have any other friends.

In sixth grade, our country-kid school gets shut down for black mold and for the ceiling leaking and they start growing mushrooms out of it, and we get sent 15 miles away to a townie school that has 300 students in a town of 1400 people.

Boykin gets held back and we're in the same class and Boykin beats me one-on-one at recess for the second time all year and then he's in reading class before the bell rings and he's telling Katie and Quinn and Kim and Tim Knutson that he always kicks my ass and makes me cry.

He's supposed to be in math class, but he hates math because Mr. Nemic is racist and hates him because he's black and so Boykin tries to fuck with the old racist anytime he can.

According to Boykin, anyway.

I walk in and he's sitting on top of my desk and they're all surrounding my desk because Tim sits behind me and hates me because I'm the new country kid and he says he's better at basketball than me and I keep challenging him to one-on-one and he won't play me.

The whole school already knows Boykin because he's the only black kid in the school besides his two sisters and they know how much he hates most teachers because—small town or out in the boonies—in Northernass Wisconsin they're all racist.

Hey Boykin, why'd old Nemic give you detention again? Cuz he's a racist ass old cracker.

Hey Boykin, Why'd you get held back? Cuz I'm black and y'all are whack.

I tap Boykin on the shoulder from behind and say that's my seat. And: Aren't you supposed to be in math right now?

He says, Ah poor whiteboy get his ass whooped by the black kid and now it's get to the back of the bus?

No, I say. It's whiteboy lets the black kid win to feel better about flunking sixth grade.

You little... he says and jumps off the desk and punches me in the face.

He may have two older sisters, one of whom uses a bat, but I have two older brothers who have both hit me in the face with bats and shovels and regularly take turns torturing me to their own delights.

I smile and say, That all you got, flunky?

He punches me again.

I smile and say, Ooh, flunky hits like a girl.

The bell rings and I say, It's time for class, Boykin. You don't want to flunk again. Then I shove him, not hard, but he's back against a desk and he falls all the way over and Kim and Quinn and Katie and even Tim start laughing and I'm waiting for Boykin to come back and beat the shit out of me, but the second bell rings and Mrs. Tibbets comes in and asks: Matthew aren't you supposed to be in math right now? And Boykin says, oh, yeah, and runs out.

We never fight.

We play one-on-one and I win the first game and Boykin wins the second game and then I win the third game and then the bell rings and Boykin tells everyone I cheated and I'm a hacker-ass scrub-honky redneck.

In seventh grade, my oldest brother kills himself.

Boykin comes to the wake. He's the only one from my class who shows up.

I sit in a back room with juice and cookies and try not to cry and Boykin distracts by telling a couple of other older kids about the time he almost kicked my ass.

I punched him and I punched him and this whiteass honky just sits there and smiles at me with this big goofy smile.

Don't you have math class, Boykin? Boykin says in a nasal whiteboy voice. You honkyass motherfucker, he says.

Eventually, he gets up to leave, but before he does, he says, Man, shit's fucked up and pats me on the back.

In eighth grade, a new kid moves to town and he is six-two and plays basketball and immediately everybody who plays basketball hates him for being six-two in seventh grade.

He wears a bowl cut and has bad acne and immediately we all start calling him penis.

His real name is Keith and he's not really a dick but he does have hairy legs and can even grow a mustache so nobody really feels bad over calling him penis.

Until Tim Anderson decides one day that he hates me more than Keith and turns pretty much the whole class against me for calling Keith penis.

Boykin isn't on the basketball team. He can't make the grades. And he doesn't really hang out with us anyway because he's a year older and we get to play basketball and he doesn't.

But then Tim tells him about me calling Keith penis and how I think I'm the best basketball player in the grade and how they should teach me a lesson.

Tim challenges me to one-on-one at the youth center one night but as soon as we start playing he starts shoving me every time I make a move. He kicks out my legs from behind when I go by him. He elbows me in the kidneys when I shoot.

When it's his ball, he puts his head down and tries to run me over while also elbowing me in the face.

Boykin is there too and he's laughing his ass off.

Kick his honky ass, Boykin yells. Tim is redheaded and pale as mayonnaise.

Keith is there too laughing awkwardly like the kid at the party who doesn't really get the joke.

C'mon motherfucker, Tim says and whips the ball at my head. Let's settle this outside.

I refuse. I say, six-two me. I say check the ball. Inside I'm ready to cry and my stomach feels rotten.

I'm not thinking about Boykin punching me in the face and then me pushing him over a desk.

I'm thinking about how I'm going to show them that I'm the best basketball player in the class.

At some point, the guy who runs the gym says he called my mom and she's coming.

Whittle baby Benny saved by his mommy, Tim says.

Boykin laughs but doesn't make any cracks at my mom's expense. Maybe out of respect for how much my mom has done for his sisters.

I only give him credit for this moment of grace looking back on it much later in our relationship.

A month later, at basketball tryouts, Boykin tells me how Tim had gotten a metal pipe and a steal chain from the alley to fuck me up big time. Boykin says, You're one lucky ass honky. All you ever want to do is play one-on-one.

This is Boykin's way of saying no hard feelings. Fuck Tim and Penis. Let's run this shit on them.

Boykin makes the team, but then gets kicked off for grades.

By our senior year, Boykin finally makes the team and keeps his grades up long enough to keep playing.

He smokes a pack a day and smokes weed most nights and doesn't play defense so he's relegated to scrub team. With me.

I have severe anxiety and every time I try to shoot in an actual game I choke.

But in practice we're the dynamic duo of the scrub team.

I play defense and dish dimes and Boykin shoots and together we make the first team run so many suicides they hate us even more than Tim and Keith and the rest of them already hated us.

Tim and Keith like to joke with Boykin about how much he smokes and how high he is half the time and sometimes Boykin'll joke about how he's the only n-word in this backwardass townie school and he can't even crack the starting five.

N-word like me, I ain't play that honky bullshit. I ain't down for no zone defense. I ain't about to run the plays. Just get this n-word the ball and let me run yo' ass.

Sometimes he talks shit to Tim and Keith and the first-stringers when we're whipping their asses. Calls us Thunder and Lightning. Chocolate Thunder and White Lightning about to bring the pain.

Sometimes Tim gets so caught up in the shit-talking he'll tell Boykin under his breath, You dumbass n-word. You ain't never gonna see the floor.

You shifty little n-word. You think coach is ever gonna put your black ass in the game?

Mostly, Boykin lets him get away with it and just acts like it's part of the game. This shit-talking.

I often wonder if it should be my job as the scrapper, the point guard, the scrub-team leader, to knock Tim's ass in the bleachers. Maybe catch him upside the chin with my elbow when he tries to take it to the hole.

I don't. I scrap. I try to get in Tim's face and be annoying. I imagine him getting so pissed off at me he hauls off and decks me and I just smile at him and then look at Boykin and we share a knowing laugh about it all.

But mostly I just try to outplay him for both of me and Boykin's sake.

Then one day it's senior night and Boykin and I actually get into the game and I turn the ball over and shoot an air ball and Boykin shoots an air ball from about five feet behind the three line and the guy he's guarding gets eight points on him in about a minute.

In the huddle coach is ripping our asses a new one as if we matter and aren't senior-year scrub team lame ducks who'll never see the floor again.

From behind the huddle, Tim whispers in Boykin's ear, You hear that? Coach ain't about that n-word ball.

It's Boykin who turns to haul off on Tim. We're up 20 points. The crowd is quiet. All anybody's watching now is Boykin trying to punch Tim and me holding him back and saying it ain't worth it and the other players holding Tim back and saying he ain't worth it.

And coach telling me to get Boykin the fuck out of here.

And me pulling Boykin away and hugging Boykin the way guys like us only feel comfortable hugging other guys—when it's under the threat of violence.

Me hugging Boykin all the way back to the locker room, the whole time him yelling: Get off me, bitch. Get the fuck off me.

Obviously Boykin gets kicked off. Nothing happens to Tim.

We have two games left and then playoffs.

I don't ever say shit to Coach or to Tim.

We lose in the first round and I never see the floor.

Boykin stops showing up to school for good after that, the final nail in his academic coffin.

I don't know if Boykin ever graduated. Maybe he got a GED, maybe he didn't.

It's not like we ever had a moment. It's not like we ever had an understanding. It's not like we were ever even friends.

I never said shit about Tim calling Boykin the n-word or about how blatantly racist everybody was to Boykin, even if Boykin always tried to joke it away.

In my head I thought it'd've going soft on him. It'd be like me throwing a game of one-on-one to him. Like if I'd pretended that he'd hurt me back then, the time he punched me. Let him save face in front of all the condescending white girls who'd never date him. White girls and white Tim and white me. And the white reading teacher.

All just to make Boykin feel like he had at least one thing up on all the rest of us. As if he'd ever needed anything from a scrubbyass honky like me.

KELLYKELLYKELLY

THERE'S THAT ONE EPISODE of *Cheers* where Woody tries to woo a young woman named Kelly to be his girlfriend.

The whole song is: *KellyKellyKellyKellyKellyKellyKelly / KellyKellyKellyKellyKelly / K-E-L-L-Y / Why? / Because you're my KellyKellyKellyKellyKelly...*

People sometimes say I look like Woody Harrelson. Not the *Cheers* Woody Harrelson with the mullet fresh off the bus from Indiana.

More like the *White Man Can't Jump* Woody.

Or sometimes, though less complimentary, more troublesomely, the *Natural Born Killers* shaved-head Woody.

Because I've shaved my head since my mom'd let me start cutting my own hair in sixth grade.

And people have told me I have some kind of crazy eye.

And I think maybe our noses. I've broken mine twice, so I don't know what that says about Woody's.

Or maybe it's our jacked-up teeth. Our crooked smiles. Our janky smirks.

But here's the thing: I'm no Woody Harrelson when it comes to women.

I do not have his right-off-the-farm harmless affability or dopey pothead charm.

His way of words.

His ability to play piano.

The first girl I give my number to was Kelly.

I don't sing her a song.

I write it on a five-dollar bill.

As tip for a corndog basket with onion rings.

She's 15 and wors at A&W.

With roller skates and a little paper hat.

It isn't a kink of mine or anything.

But it isn't not hot either.

She's black.

Or maybe mixed race.

Is mixed-race offensive?

I mean aren't all people who are part black just *black* black?

Isn't this the moral of all of us white people learning to be less racist about Obama than every other racist white person.

(Though on the other hand, half the rednecks I went to school with claimed to be 1/16 Native American so they could feel better about making Lone Ranger and Tonto jokes and maybe get a scholarship for college.)

I've only recently learned that *mulatto* is an offensive term.

Mulatto being the quote-unquote *correct terminology* we learn from history class in Northernass Wisconsin.

Which should've been the first clue it was offensive.

The second clue being my boss calling Kelly a mulatto the first time we see her at A&W.

I don't know what Kelly would've called herself up in Northernass Wisconsin in the late 90s.

My boss, on the other hand, is the kind of redneck who calls himself *Dinger*.

He's a real cum-dinger, ain't he? That is just one of Dingers many jokes about why he calls himself Dinger.

Another one is: *A real cum-dinger, don'tcha know?*

His full name Garibald (Gary) Kundinger II.

Technically he's just my supervisor, not my actual boss (Even in Northernass Wisconsin, I don't know if you're allowed to be the boss if you call yourself Dinger).

The best thing I can say about Dinger is that he takes us to A&W for lunch when he is extra hungover and wants to watch a bunch of teenage girls on roller skates.

And Dinger's often hungover.

I work for a natural gas company.

My job's to *walk the line* to make sure there were no natural gas leaks seeping up out of the ground.

I'm never told what we're supposed to do if something's about to blow up.

We have a little pocket notebook like cops to take notes and walkie-talkies that almost never work.

One of many reasons to question Dinger's authority.

Mostly Dinger's job as *supervisor* is to sit in the car while my partner and I walk and then drive us back home at the end of the day.

Babysitting, he calls it.

Dinger and I like A&W for slightly different reasons.

My reason is Kelly.

His reason: pretty much any woman who's got them *tig-o-bitties* (as he likes to say).

I have to give this to Dinger—he's an equal opportunity leerer of *tig-o-bitties*.

They could be perky high school tig-o-bitties. They could be single-mom-of-three-kids-with-three baby-daddies stretch-marked tig-o-bitties. They could be six-months pregnant tig-o-bitties.

Dinger's favorite, this lady who manages A&W, and not what you'd call conventionally attractive. Tig-o-bitties like dried-out unrisen loaves of yeasty bread dough.

But to Dinger she's got them tig-o-bitties and that's enough, which I kind of admire in a that's still fucked-up kind of way.

I'm 45 now and weigh 300 pounds and look like Woody Harrelson if Woody Harrelson had eaten both Cliff and Norm from *Cheers*.

What I wouldn't give to be objectified? Even if it was someone saying I'd give my left nut to motorboat my tig-o-man-bitties.

Even if it was a guy like Dinger.

Have I mentioned all the jungle-fever jokes I get about Kelly?

Hey Benny boy, you better wear extra protection out there on the line today. All those swamps and skeeters out there, you don't watch out you'll end up with a nasty case of that jungle fever.

Hey Benny boy, you itching to go to A&W today? You know that they call that itch, right? It's that jungle fever, boy.

Huh, huh, I say.

What I don't say: *That shit ain't funny, Ding.*

Not: *Yo, that's straight up racist bullshit, man. You know that?*

Not: *Have you even seen the movie?*

What I say: *You're the fucking worst, Dinger.*

This my pathetic gutless way of making it known that Dinger is fucked up, but in an eye-rolly, *oh you rascal* kind of way that really just enables him.

But of course, if I were to say something, then he'd stop going to A&W just to piss me off.

Basically A&W and flirting with Kelly > anti-racism.

She ain't got no tits, that one, he tells me.

Says things like: *Really? That one? Her? But she ain't got no tits, little buddy? No hips on her. No junk in the trunk? You think she even got any grass on the putting green?*

Me saying: *Please stop.*

Dinger: *The founding member of the itty-bitty itty committee?*

Me saying all huffy: *Well, no offense, Dinger, but I ain't all about them tig-o-bitties like you.*

This, officially the most I ever stand up to Dinger while I work there.

You think five is enough? I ask him. *Or 10? 20?*

That girl? Dinger says. *I wouldn't pay that girl to…*

I won't tell you what he says next. Should I have given her the 20 and not been able to eat at all which seemed more awkward and creepy somehow?

Should I have given her the 10 and split the difference (*all about the benjamins baby!*) but then I wouldn't've been able to afford the banana split I always got. The one she'd always call me out for: *And one banana split, extra cherries for you, Hon?*

Which is my favorite thing about Kelly from A&W—the *Hon* part. The extra cherries free of charge part.

I decide to go cheap.

And she never calls me.

And probably it serves me right.

But now I'm left to wonder if she ever even looked at the five-dollar bill or if she just split tips or changed out for something bigger and now my number is just floating around who knows what sketchy bar or greasy spoon or graffitied truck stop bathroom in Northernass Wisconsin.

I eventually look up her number.

It's basketball season and we're about to play her team. The team she cheerleads for. The team her brother plays for, her brother the same age as me, her brother, also black/mixed race who hates me from the time he first catches me checking out his sister while taking the ball out of bounds.

Gimme a P! Gimme an E! Gimme an R! Gimme a V!

What's that spell?

I'm not sure how I convince myself that I'm going to manage the brother situation, but I decide it's time to shoot my shot.

The phone book lists it as Kelly and Robert Burke.

Which confuses me:

Is her mother named Kelly too? Like Kelly II?

Is that such a thing for girls?

And who will I ask for if Mr. Burke picks up the phone?

If her brother picks up the phone?

Do I ask for Little Kelly? (which sounds somewhat offensive)

Kelly Jr.? (which sounds absurd)

Maybe: *Ms.* Kelly not *Mrs.* (which sounds completely pompous)

I finally grow a pair and call her the week before the game.

A guy answers.

It's not her brother.

Presumably Robert. (Or Bob? Or Rob? Bert? Her brother's name being Robbie, so…?)

I ask for Kelly.

He says she's not here. Can I take a message? Who's this?

He doesn't say anything about a mom or a daughter or that Kelly's at work and has no time for boys.

Does he know that I've been the one that Robbie has caught smiling at her during an out-of-bound play?

Does he somehow hear it in my voice?

I hang up.

I've probably missed my window anyway. I'm a senior and then off to college. I'm not going to be the creeper college boy dating a high school sophomore and going to homecoming and holding hands at the football game and all that.

The big thing is I won't be working summers with Dinger and walking the line anymore. That's a high school gig.

It's all pretty heartbreaking to me.

Things don't get better when I see her at the game.

Do I purposely go diving for that ball into the bleachers where Kelly and the rest of the cheerleaders were?

What kind of magic/luck that my head would somehow end up right between Kelly's legs?

To this day, I can only tell you that guilt is all about context. And point of view.

And from her brother's point of view staring at me with my head up her skirt, it doesn't matter how effusively I can apologize. To him or her.

I can understand a big brother not wanting his kid sister to have some sweaty guy falling between her legs and then winking at her.

I can especially understand a black/mixed-race brother not wanting a white shaved-head wannabe like me falling between the legs of his black/mixed-race sister.

We end up beating his team by 20 points.

But as they say, there's winning the battle and losing the war.

And that's the last time we play them.

My last shot.

And I blow it.

Or rather I take a dive.

And never see or hear from her again.

Not that I'd done anything to deserve her.

But does she ever think of me after that (the way that I've too often thought of her)?

Is there something triggering in even the most random reference to the exploits of Ben Affleck? Benedict Cumberbatch? Sir Ben Kingsley?

Oh that reminds me, I wonder whatever happened to that sweet innocent dopey Ben who once tipped me his telephone number on the back of a five-dollar bill and thought I would call him back?

Maybe the latest Woody Harrelson movie or TV show or interview about legalizing marijuana for everyone?

That goofy grin. Those crazy eyes. All that charm oozing out of his every weed-stinking pore.

Just last week Woody went on *Saturday Night Live* and gave a rambling impromptu opening monologue where he compared the government mandating Covid vaccinations to a drug cartel forcing everybody to take drugs.

I think to myself: What's more fucked up—that Woody's so stoned all the time that he thinks that the government is a drug cartel? Or the insinuation is that Mexican drug lords who are parading through our borders to take over the country?

Who knows what Woody's thinking at any time these days and why any of us would care what Woody's conspiracy theories are, I don't know.

Another aging white male movie star with strong opinions about how the world is going to shit.

This all being what I think about whenever I think about my first broken heart.

KellyKellyKellyKellyKelly / K-E-L-L-Y / Why? / Because you were never gonna be mine.

MR. GOOD SAMARITAN

HALFWAY ACROSS THE BRIDGE there's a dead body blocking the walkway.
 Or maybe it's one of those where some serial killer just pretends to be a dead body only to trick you and slit your throat—*A ha! Gotcha motherfucker!*
 I watch a lot of *Dateline*.
 This is why I hesitate a bit to lean in and check to see if it's dead or needs help.
 On cue, it sits up like a zombie and shoots me—*p'ew, p'ew, I got you.*
 I don't die.
 It's not dead.
 They're finger guns.
 He looks Native American.
 I catch my breath.
 I steady my hands.
 I offer a hand.
 You need a hand, buddy? I say.
 He laughs.
 Nah, man. I'm cool. I'm cool.
 He looks out over the edge of the bridge where his feet are dangling.
 Just look at that shit, man.
 Just look at that shit, man.
 Yeah, man, I say.
 P'ew, p'ew, p'ew, he says. I gotcha yah.
 I say yeah you got me.
 I'm already stepping over him and walking away. I don't want to get shot.
 I'm hungover.
 Going to be late for work.
 No coat.

The wind coming off the lake, shaking my bones.

My walk of shame back to my place, wherever I've parked my Bronco.

Hey! he hollers back at me.

Hey! I holler back, only half turning around.

You got any money?

I don't have any money. It's the truth.

I make a thing out of patting my pockets and then shrug.

Sorry, man, nah, I say.

It's cool, he says. It's cool.

Then he shoots me with the finger guns one more time: P'ew, p'ew, he says. I gotcha.

I grab my heart and make a dying face. You got me, I say. You got me. I smile big.

Then he lies back down like a Native American zombie on rewind.

His legs swaying ever so slightly over the side of the bridge.

It could be the wind, it could be a sign of life.

It could be a cry for help, it could be he just loves life from above.

It could be he needs mental treatment, it could be he's just homeless and happy.

Who's to judge?

I'm in no position to judge.

Judge not that you get judged first.

Let he who casts the first stone live in a glass house.

Something like that.

It's in the bible.

JOY

I LOSE MY VIRGINITY TO JOY.
    This is not a euphemism.
    This is not an allegory.
    This might actually be an allegory.
    This is me, Mister Big-Time Loser, age 22.
    As much as a 22-year-old can *lose* his virginity.
    When it's a gift.
    Perhaps less of a gift for Joy.
    She calls me Coach B.
    Coach B despite the fact that I'm actually the ball boy.
    Or maybe in spite of.
    Maybe a little joke at my expense.
    Coach B for *Because I'm the Ball Boy.*
    But also because: *Ben.*
    Coach B, what do I do?
    Joy is not a player.
    But has done it with most of the players I fetch balls for.
    The players I see naked on a daily basis while collecting sweatyass stinking jockstraps, jerseys, socks, and undies.
    Though I don't know this at the time.
    What do I do, Coach? What do I do? What do I do?
    When the condom slips off.
    And the second one slips off.
    Gets lost up there, stuck, whatever you might call it.
    Obviously, I'm no expert on navigating the nooks and crannies of the female anatomy.
    It's not that she's a large woman.
    With no magical vaginal powers that I know of.
    Though I have no other comparisons for how small or large or magical her vagina might be.
    Third time's a charm? I say.

I've made the mistake of borrowing my roommate's prophylactics.

He's black.

His name's Q.

For Quincy.

I've seen more than my share of black dicks while collecting dirty, sweaty jocks.

Can I testify?

It's true, the rumors, the jokes.

Stereotypes always have at least a pinky toe dipped in the truth.

My roommate Q might as well have his face on the back of the box.

The subtitle: *The Magnum Man!*

It's a Sunday.

Six in the morning.

Mother's Day.

The symbolism of it all is not in my favor.

I call the only person I can think to call at six in the morning.

I don't call G.

I call the nurse hotline.

An angry nurse sighs.

No, the emergency room does not take lost condoms.

Unless they involve larger, potentially dangerous objects. (e.g. lost vibrators or light bulbs or small boa constrictors)

Well, how long has it been?

How many of them are up there?

No, the Morning After is not just for the morning after.

The morning after the morning after will do just fine.

What do I do, Coach? Tell me what to do? What do I do, Coach?

I'm full of answers after the news of a Plan B.

Joy still has questions:

What do I do with you, Coach B?

Which pretty soon becomes:

What do you want me to do to you, Coach B?

It's amazing how quickly a last second turnover can become sweating it out in a triple-overtime thriller.

With the right perspective.

And a well-timed timeout.

Sorry, I say afterward, I swear I've never done this type of thing before.

And you think I've ever done this type of thing?

She's holding up Q's freshly opened box of prophylactics: ten-pack, seven left.

Oh she's done this type of thing before, Q says afterward.

This type of thing and that type of thing and the other.

Pretty much all the things.

With all the players.

And all the coaches.

How you think she worked her way down to you?

You ain't exactly the top seed, B.

With Joy, you best watch out, boy, he tells me.

Mess around too much you won't be calling her Joy for long.

When Joy comes a'knocking nine months later looking for Child Support.

Which I think is pretty sexist.

Not the least of because I'm 22 years old.

And horny.

And pent up.

A virgin until quite recently.

And ready to believe the best in any girl who'd have sex with me.

Twenty-two years of training for this day.

Twenty-two years looking for Joy.

And now I've found her.

And one morning after one morning I've lost her.
Joy never to've come a'knocking again.
Does she ever go through with it?
Shouldn't it be Plan AB for Anti-Baby?
Joy never having called me Coach B again.
Would she even remember what I'd taught her—days, months, years later?
With her future players? Teammates? Ballboys? Coach B's and D's?
Or BD's.
(aka Baby Daddies).
The true gifts from god.
Sometimes, sadly, just a regift.
As with every other Joy that gets lost in search of Plan B.

Q

Q TELLS ME they'll either think I'm five-oh or *White Men Can't Jump*.

He doesn't laugh or smile.

I've been called Woody Harrelson before, but mostly by old people and obnoxious drunk old people.

Woody Harrelson is not the most attractive man I wouldn't say, but then neither am I.

I don't think I look like a five-oh, but then as a white guy I don't really get to decide if I look like a five-oh to black people.

We're on our way down to the cities listening to my mix of old school Tribe, De la Souls, etc., my contribution to our journey along with my car.

I'm being careful to show Q I know all the words, but also know *all the words*.

I've half-jokingly asked Q before if it's okay for me to sing along if it's just the words of the song.

He unjokingly confirmed it is not.

I don't remember why we were going to the cities to get Q a hair cut; I don't remember why I am with him.

We're cool and all.

Live together.

Work together.

I'm just not the type of Q friend that goes with him to the barber shop.

This is where things get complicated for me telling you this story.

We were going to the barber shop. We were listening to Pac. We stopped off at Popeyes.

Sometimes *showing* can seem more racist than *telling*.

But I love all those things too.

Barber shop to trim up my fade? Yes please.

Bump Pac the whole way up? Yes, I did.

Popeyes? Who doesn't like fried chicken?

And yes, Q is a former college basketball star while I am a former college basketball scrub/team walkon.

And if this was *White Men Can't Jump*, you better bet we'd hustle you (or rather, Q would hustle you and I would set a lot of picks, get a lot of rebounds, and probably get punched by your best player for hustling too much and get that player either ejected or arrested), but a hustle would happen.

G doesn't give me any directions on what to say or not say at the barber shop. He says, you'll be alright. Or rather, he says *ah-ight*.

Then he says the thing about *White Men Can't Jump* or five-oh.

It's the five-oh part that hurts my feelings.

He's cracking up big time at that one and I'm cracking up too, it's a good joke, but also a little scared too, which then makes me feel kind of racist for being scared of going to the barber shop with a black friend to get his do fresh.

But Q's not really talking to me. He's on his blue-tooth hittin up his previous roommate Antoine who goes by Toine and sometimes just T.

Why is it fucked up that I feel racist even writing that this dude's name was Toine? Again with the showing versus telling.

e.g. I don't see color. I just see a collection of black stereotypes that make me sound racist in my descriptions even if they're true.

No, no, I totally *don't get off* on the fact that despite my honkyness, Q calls me B.

Here's a thing: Q's real name is Quincy lives and works with me in Northernass Wisconsin (an hour away from where I grew up), but hails from Toronto. He's a coach, I'm the manager.

Sometimes we play two on two with guys from the team who get mouthy about foul calls or having to do drills, or sometimes the guys making fun of me for being a grownass man as *ball boy* as they call me.

We take bets for running suicides or for who has to do laundry for the practice gear that week?

And Q always has my back.

The same way I always have Q's back when we're standing for the National Anthem and he's worried that two or more of his girlfriends might show up to the game and sit next to each other.

My job is lookout. Maybe run a little interference once in a while. Tell one of them that Q likes it when she sits in a certain spot so he can see her during the game.

The way Q had my back when I didn't have a condom so I took one of Q's and then the condom fell off because it was a magnum and I was not a magnum and now I'd possibly impregnated a random basketball groupie named Joy.

But he said, Nah, you'll be ah-ight. Because it was probably just pre-cum and if a girl's having sex with a dude like you and isn't on the pill, that's on her.

Which isn't the way my mom raised me to think about girls and pregnancy, but my mom wasn't there and when one is worried about screwing up their entire future by getting a rando pregnant over an oversized condom, it's easy to forget one's ideals about feminism and personal responsibility.

One time Q called me in the middle of me interviewing to be promoted to assistant coach to tell me that he was gonna have one of his girls over that afternoon and I needed to come home and clean up the dooty I'd left around the toilet bowl.

One time Q called me because his main girlfriend's mom had gotten in a car accident. She'd been rushing to the hospital with her husband who was already dying of cancer but having a bad night.

A drunk driver going the wrong way down a one-way street with no lights on.

The mother killed instantly. The dad dying a month later of cancer.

What do I even fucking say to her? Q wanted to know. What do you even tell someone after some shit like that happens?

I imagine he called me because my brother had killed himself when I was 12.

I imagine he called me because I had accidentally burned my house down when I was fourteen.

Maybe also because I was white and his girl was white and there's a whole different mentality to grief when you're privileged and white but bad shit still happens.

That's why we were going to the barbers, I realize now.

It was old girl's dad's funeral the next day.

Old girl, what Q called his main girl.

I won't tell you her real name, I won't blow up Q's spot, even 20 years later, but I will tell you that it was a whiteassed name but that he called her J sometimes too.

Or there was the time when I tried messing with three different girls at the same time to impress G, but I couldn't handle it.

You need your starter, your sixth man, and your bench warmer for team morale.

In Q's life I knew my role and I knew it well.

Q was like, Dawg, not all playas are made for this game.

Ain't that right, Toine, he said into his blue tooth.

And I was like, shit. You don't have to tell me, dawg.

Woody Harrelson's dad was a hit man. He was the first man in the twentieth century to murder a federal judge.

He married five times and abandoned Woody when he was seven years old.

If I were Woody Harrelson and he was my dad, I don't know if I'd've played that role in *Natural Born Killers*, but on the other hand, maybe that was the role he was born to play.

If Woody Harrelson had not been in *Natural Born Killers*, he would've starred in *A Time to Kill* based on the John Grisham book.

Imagine if instead of Matthew McConaughey, Woody Harrelson had delivered that monologue at the end about the black girl getting raped and then saying: *imagine if she was white.*

Those crazy eyes. That broken nose. That crooked-toothed smile.

It probably wouldn't have played as well.

The same way that my crazy eyes, broken nose, and crooked smile don't play very well in a black barbershop or as the assistant coach of many black basketball players.

I ended up messing around with Q's girl a couple months after her parents dying.

Q and her had already been on the outs. He'd come clean about his sixth-man girl and bench warmer—though assured her that she'd been his go-to player.

It's not like it was all too crude of a comparison. J had been a star basketball player too, albeit white.

I may be attracted to people who have gone through horrible trauma. They may be attracted to me.

When I listened to my first Tupac CD when I was a kid, I immediately felt like I knew what he was talking about.

I didn't. I didn't know shit about what any of the shit he was talking about.

But I knew death and houses burning down and trauma and anger and sadness and a dark sense of humor.

And maybe that's why I've always been a wannabe. Why I've always been the one trying to tag along with the Q's of this world.

Which is a fucked-up thing, I know it.

But it's true too.

That's probably what brought J and I together in the first place, or at least what kept us trying for the two months we did:

We both desperately wanted Q's approval.

As far as I know, Q grew up with a dad and a mom and never lost a close friend or family member, never went to jail, and never sold drugs.

It's fucked up when those are the credentials listed to support the argument that Q was not your stereotypical black man.

Do I have more street cred because my brother killed himself and I burned down my house (even though we had insurance to build a whole new house)? Or that my old lady would die of a heart attack five years later.

What about J and her parents and how fucked up that was?

What do I even say to her about something like that? he'd asked me.

How the fuck am I supposed to know? Just because my brother killed himself and I burned down my family's house?

That's not what I said. That's what I thought.

And for a moment I thought that this must be what it's like when white people ask black people how to feel when black people get murdered by the cops or sent to prison for things they didn't do.

Just for a moment I thought that. Then I thought what a fucked-up thing to think. As if my trauma is some sort of privilege.

I haven't spoken to Q since the year I gave up on coaching and moved away.

Twenty years now.

I think the thing that hurt the most was the last time I came back.

The next me had moved in with Q. The team manager, white guy, wannabe with the Nike gear and the hip hop mixes.

This is not an exaggeration. This is not a joke how all black people think white people look the same.

What's up, Q? What's crackin?

Oh you know how I do. I do. I do. You met D, here? Shit y'all should know each other. Y'all would get along for sure. Hey D, tell Ben here about us having to ball up after practice the other day?

Did D have a better jumper than me? Did D have better handle? He had me by a couple inches, ten, 15 pounds of muscle.

What's up, brah? he says to me. Pulls me in to dap him. Q said I had some big shoes to fill.

Did D hustle like me? Did D set picks and pass the ball like me?

I hadn't picked up a ball since I'd left. Probably I'd already put on twenty pounds since then.

Look at you, boy, Q said. You been eatin good now ain't you?

I asked if he'd heard from J. If he knew where she'd ended up. I knew she'd left, but it's not like we'd kept in touch. The white-people trauma aside, our real connective tissue had always been Q.

Nah, Q said. I ain't heard from ol' girl in a long time. You ain't? Honestly, I thought y'all would end up together, everything you had in common.

Everything we'd had in common.

I was a walk-on team scrub turned team manager/adult ball boy.

She'd been the star of her team. Been the assistant coach the same way Q had been assistant coach.

The fact that she'd ever hooked up with a scrub like me in the first place tells you enough about what we had in common.

I wanted to ask Q about his new recruiting class, his lady squad—the starter, the sixth-man, the bench-warmer. I wanted to live vicariously through sexual exploits if only one last time.

I wanted to ask Q about the *team*-team, who'd mouthed off about who and what, and what the deal was with this new guy Drew, my replacement. Did they even interview him or did they just catch the dude playing ball one day and tab him as Woody 2.0.

He didn't look anything like Woody to me, but then again, I'm white. I don't think I look like Woody. I'm just willing to take it if that's what gets me a chick here and there or an invitation to a pickup game.

I wanted to have Q tell me that things hadn't been the same without me. *Yo, you gotta know that D ain't no B, I'll tell you that much.*

I waited. I listened. Out of self-presentation I didn't pay much attention.

Things were cool. Things were cool.

For both of us.

He didn't miss me and I didn't miss him.

But everything was cool.

I didn't have no shorty.

He didn't have no shorty.

He hadn't married J just to help some girl cope with horrible trauma.

He hadn't married me just to help some dude cope with being nothing without him.

No groupies, he used to tell me. No hangers on.

You gotta keep it real with these girls. They gotta know there's nothing else going on here. It's a transactional agreement. You get yours, they get theirs. Nobody gets hurt.

Try to be nice to everybody and not hurt their feelings, you end up the asshole anyway. Except you're even worse. Because you pretended not to be the asshole from the beginning.

That was the thing Q taught me. I was the asshole. The blue-eyed, blond-haired, *Natural Born* asshole.

SHONDA

IT'S ONE OF THOSE BARS with the black lights and too much neon and so much stale cigarette smoke. Through all that yellow and green and blue and purple haze, oh the shapes they make.

These the largest women of town dancing with their skinniest men. The badunkadunk bump and grind and back that ass up. Beep, beep, beep like so many Zamboni machines.

I'm not a skinny enough man for large women to want to steamroll me, but I'm a connoisseur of both the World Wildlife Foundation and the World Wrestling Federation.

I'm alone in a corner booth. Sporting my finest suit. I have one suit. It's from JC Penney's.

I've had maybe six Captain Cokes.

A large woman comes sliding in next to me. Suddenly there's not enough table to go around.

She puts her hand on my thigh and whisper-shouts, *Baby, baby* in my ear. The bar vibrating with bass and drum machines to the pitter patter of my tender heart.

Shonda, she whisper-shouts in my ear.

What? I shout-whisper back.

She smells like coconut and weed and B.O.

If Shonda'd been the prostitute, I'd've paid her my life savings. My life savings amounting to 42 dollars and 27 cents. Give or take six Captain-Cokes at booty bar prices.

I feel a little misogynistic for thinking Shonda might've been the prostitute. Instead of the pimp. The pimp I will later learn her to be.

What's a baby like you doing in a place like this? she says.

Oh, baby, I want to say, I'm not a baby. Or a man. I'm the team manager for the college basketball team.

I'm what they call the ballboy when you're 25 years old. When your job is fetching big bouncy balls for other bigger bouncier men.

That's what they call you when you wear a suit to the game to keep stats at the end of the bench. When you wear the same suit out to the club after the game. Like a real perv.

But does Shonda need to know this? No, she does not.

We make out for a little bit. Then stop.

Like what you see, baby?

I like what I see.

But Shonda's purposely misleading me. Does not mean what I see in her. She's meaning what I now see in this model-skinny white chick in white pants.

It's always the one in white pants that gets you.

Is this one of those gotcha questions? I've never been good with girls and their gotcha questions. Or women.

But I've never met so much woman as Shonda.

See how ol' girl's looking at you, baby?

Ol' girl is maybe 19, 20, 21 going on 42. Half-heartedly gyrating to a deep cut off Master P's greatest hits. Sipping a blue drink from a long straw in a tall glass.

As far as I can see through the haze cigarette smoke and neon, White-Pants Girl has eyes only for the straw of her blue drink.

She is the bell of the ball. The menagerie of all shapes and sizes of hot flesh melting in around her. So much woman flesh, so little man bones. So much bump and grind and adoration.

The whole thing is a major fire hazard. In everyone's pants but mine.

Five hundred, Shonda whisper-shouts.

I look at Shonda, I look at White-Pants Girl.

Five hundred, baby, she's all yours.

I'm confused. I am taken aback. More than a little heartbroken. I don't believe my ears.

I would've given my life savings to keep making out with Shonda. But I played it cool.

Nah, I whisper in Shonda's voluptuous ear, I'm cool.

If I'd been truly cool, I'd've told Shonda: Nah, baby, nah, I'm cool. You's all the woman I need. Then palm her big bubble butt and stick my tongue down her tonsils like a gentleman.

I do not tell her about my life savings.

Okay, you got me, baby, she whisper-shouts in my ear.

Let's say 400. Call it my special honey baby man discount.

Nah, nah, I say, I'm cool.

I am not cool.

Baby, baby, baby, she says. What are you doing to me?

She's motioning for White-Pants Girl to come hither but White-Pants Girl can't see us for all the bump and grind.

If I am ever to become a basketball coach, I will have to get better at these recruiting events.

Shonda's strong sweaty hand back on my thigh, cherry red fingernails inching closer to my inner thigh.

I would've given my life savings for her cherry red fingernails to keep on inching up to my three-and-a-half inches.

Three hundo, she says, but you're taking advantage of me now, baby.

I'm regretting my decision to leave my tab open.

Shit, dude, two-fifty is straight up insulting to ol' girl, but that can stay between you and me, baby.

I am doing the *check please* sign, trying to flag down any server I can find. This is not a bar with servers. Things are starting to turn ugly.

Now you're cute and all, baby, just who you think talking to?

I can feel her sweet spittle tickling my ear.

You come down here in your fancy little suity-suit…

I can feel her fingernails digging in.

Just check out dat ass, baby. Now I know you don't think you're too good for dat ass, baby? Two hundred for dat ass? Not even for you, baby. One-fifty?

Against my better judgment I'm shuffling my thighs away from her sharp red nails. Against my better judgment I'm pissing my Shonda right the fuck off.

Fuck, baby, you think you can get ass like that on gratis?

White-Pants Girl here now, appearing out of the smoke and lights like POOF!

Shonda's fingernails walking up and down the curve of that white-pants ass. The cherry red fingernails that should've been running up and down the cotton-twill of my suited inner thighs.

Well, fuck me, then, she's saying.

And I'm saying, Yes please.

White-Pants Girl isn't speaking. White-Pants Girl drinking her blue drink from her long straw. Staring off at the dance floor, the black lights, the few couples left bumping and grinding. White-Pants Girl like a labradoodle who won't pose for the family photo.

I feel guilty for thinking of White-Pants Girl like a labradoodle. I'm sure she was a perfectly nice sweet girl who'd had a tough childhood full of dirty jeans and bloody knees.

Not that prostitutes can't have healthy non-traumatic childhoods and still be prostitutes. Or call girls. Sex workers. Escorts. I'm not sure what the appropriate nomenclature is now.

How many drinks would they charge me for if I just cut and run? Forty-two bucks to some is five hundred to others.

You must think you're some fine catch, huh? Mister Suit Man. What you even doing here if you don't wanna party? Mister Suit Man.

If she only knew what a ballboy I truly was. If she only knew the type of physical specimens I fetched balls for.

Nah, nah, nah…

My suit butt is making swishy-squeaky noises as I try to scoot toward the other side of the booth. I'm not making much headway with Shonda. She's got me by the arm now. It's getting sexier and scarier.

I would've given her my life savings to make her let me go. I would've given her my life savings to make her hold me tighter.

You know what you're doing to me, baby?

I've lost the ability to string together syllables.

Nah, nah, I say trying to scoot, scoot.

You know what you're making me do?

Nah, nah.

What you doing to ol' girl, here?

Nah.

You think ol' girl ain't got needs?

Nah.

You know what, fuck you, dude. You ain't even got a Benjamin on you?

This is what I'm thinking: I'm thinking, How does Shonda know my name and why is this the first time she's using it? Benjamin, Benji, Benny, Ben-Ben-Ben-Bennnnnnnnn…

My life savings for a word, one syllable, those lips, that tongue.

One bill, baby, but just the nitty-gritty. No extra-curriculars.

Why is she calling me Bill now?

This is what I'm thinking. This is the simple confusion she's driven me to.

White-Pants Girl is whispering something in her ear. Shonda shaking her head.

Nah, nah, it's cool, baby.

Now it's Shonda with mixed messages.

Now it's me with the upper hand.

Thank god, some bouncer's come to save me. He is not a skinny man.

This lady bothering you, sir?

Yes, sir, she sure is. She is *hot-and-bothering* me.

I don't say that.

I say, Nah, nah, man, I'm cool.

Shonda says, Nah, nah, we cool.

The bouncer says, What I tell you the last time, Shonda?

The bartender says, You ain't got to go home, but you gotta gets the fuck up outta here. He's not talking specifically to us, but he's not talking not to us.

White-Pants Girl has made her escape, has disappeared into the bright blinding lights of last call. Maybe she was never there to begin with. Maybe this whole time I've been mistaking the price of Shonda's love for an angel in white. Maybe this whole time I've been playing hard to get with my own wildest fantasies.

And now Shonda's let go of me. Let go of us. The light has come and Shonda does not like what she sees in me.

Man, fuck you, she says to the bouncer. And fuck this white boy, too.

I'm no longer Ben to her, I'm not even Bill. I'm nothing but an empty suit to her. A white boy who can't even fetch his own balls when the opportunity presents itself.

My bill comes to 55.74. My life savings for six watered-down Captain and Cokes. Thirteen thirty-two my debt for services unrendered. How much more I'll have to pay for coming up so short.

I ask the bouncer on the way out how well he knows Shonda. I want to know how well he knows her and how well he *knows* her.

Shonda? he says. Shit, she's always runnin game on white dudes like you.

Nah, nah, it wasn't like that.

Shit, he says. That's how Shonda gets you. See ol' girl over there? he says.

And like God Himself has pulled a rabbit out of His hat, White-Pants Girl has reappeared under the streetlights.

You don't need Shonda to get a girl like that, he says.

White-Pants Girl waving, smiling, looking enthused for the first time all night. Her white pants, her halogen halo.

Now that's my girl, he says waving back.

But yo, I tell you what, dude, he says looking me up and down. He rubs his fingers down my tie, buttons up the button on my suit.

He whisper-shouts in my ear: Five hundo and I'll let you rent her for the night.

Yeah? I say.

Best investment you'll make in your life, he says. He's waving for White-Pants Girl to come over. She's crossing the street without looking. Her white pants as if on a cloud from heaven.

And I can finally see now what Shonda sees in her, what this bouncer sees in her. And I can finally see what fate I've been futilely avoiding all night. All those big eyes following me back to my place. Pinning me down on my own bed and having their way with me.

Where's your TV, yo?

Where's your DVD?

Your wallet, bitch?

Your cash?

Your credit card?

This your only goddamn suit?

And me with nothing to offer but dirty underwear and empty pockets.

Take everything.

Whatever you need.

I've got nothing of value to offer.

But everything to give.
Do with me what you want.
Take me for what you can get.
I'll always be in your debt.
I'll always come up short.
Oh Shonda, oh Shonda.
I'm sorry, I'm sorry, I'm so so sorry.
Baby baby baby.
I'll never know another name.

TC

TC'S DAD IS TERRY CUMMINGS.

TC is also Terry Cummings, but he goes by TC for Terry Cummings instead of Terry Cummings Jr.

Terry Cummings Sr. was the NBA rookie of the year in 1983. A two-time all-star and two time all-NBA.

TC has been kicked out of three DI colleges before he ends up here. Not for drugs or partying. Mostly for being a dick to all coaches and teammates.

Up here being a tinyass no-scholarship DIII school in Northernass Wisconsin with like 15 other black people within a 50-mile radius, 10 of them playing on the team after getting kicked off other better teams for various reasons, the other five being ex-players having stuck around to live the life of five black guys surrounded by like 500 white girls who've never met or slept with a black man before.

Which I can tell you, having been in locker rooms in high school versus locker rooms in college, the myth about black men is no myth.

For instance, TC being the only black guy I'd ever met over six six, I can tell you that he is long and strong all over.

Not to mention, the closest I've ever came to NBA talent and athleticism.

Me being TC's ballboy.

But also TC's team manager, TC practice team scrub, and TC's wannabe assistant coach with no real power other than to rat on TC if he curses out anybody or tries to fight anybody and refuses to do his 20 required pushups as punishment.

Here being TC's last chance, his dad having told him he'll be paying his own way to a college education if he doesn't get his shit together.

TC's dad never actually coming to any games or practices. Just the phone calls and the texts—mostly to Coach.

Mostly for Coach to rat out TC for trying to fight any of the coaching staff or teammates. Again. For like the twentieth time.

Which basically makes me and Coach the same in being potential rats on TC.

Of course, my job is not just to rat on TC.

It's to *toughen him up* as Coach calls it.

It's to hack the shit out of him in practice drills and in scrimmages and then as practice ref to not call any fouls on other guys who hack him in practice drills and scrimmages and then to call ticky-tack fouls on him anytime he even touches another guy.

And then to tell him to get down and give me 20 pushups every time he motherfucks me when I hack him or not call a hack on him or call him for hacking somebody else.

Basically be a dick back to him.

Which is sad, really.

If it weren't for all this toughening up and the fact that I'm short white and have no talent and that he's tall and black and could play anywhere if not for hating all his coaches and teammates, I think TC and I could be the best of friends.

His dad getting on his case for getting kicked out of three different schools.

My dad getting on mine for listening to hip hop about bitches and hoes and for dressing like I was a rapper who rapped about bitches and hoes.

His little brother being a McDonald's All American going to UCLA.

My big brother hating basketball and life in general and killing himself his senior year instead of going to college at all.

Our mutual love of Tupac and Jay-Z and DMX and other rappers who rap about bitches and hoes and for dressing like rappers who rap about bitches and hoes.

Oh how the littlest of things can keep people from being the best of friends.

For TC and me, that means that sometimes I'm going to hack the living shit out of him with a tackling pad from the football team and for TC it means that sometimes he's gonna shed my tackling pad, dunk on me anyway, grab his junk, and call me a bitchass little w-n-word.

And then I'll have to tell him to give me 20.

And he'll have to tell me to suck his dick.

And I'll have to tell Coach.

And Coach'll have to call his TC Sr.

Who'll have to call TC.

Who'll have to come in the next practice and apologize for calling me a bitch-ass little w-n-word.

The sad cycle of dickishness.

Maybe I'm just a no-talent honky practice team scrub/ball boy/team manager/wannabe assistant coach, but I for one am ready to do my part to break that cycle.

Which means taking TC's shit and not saying shit to anybody.

TC throws his dirty sweaty practice undies in my face and tells me to eat shit as I walk into the locker room.

I eat that shit. I run it through the wash twice. Use my own fabric softener because the school athletic department doesn't even have any. Leave them hanging in his locker the next day before practice. A little post-it note: *Mm-mm, delicious.*

TC whips two basketballs at my face one after another as I am gathering up the basketballs at the end of practice, tells me to suck balls, *w-n-word*, I dodge one and take that the other to the face, break my nose, and go to the hospital?

I suck those balls. Show up the next day to practice with two black eyes, a face-guard that makes me look like a serial killer, and slap myself in the face-guard, tell him I'm ready to take however many balls he wants to hit me with.

TC puts moves on me in the post as I hack the shit out of him with my blocking pad, he hollers *midget on my back*! then clears me out with his elbow, knocks out my two front teeth?

I become the midget on his back. The midget with two new teeth. I come to practice the next day with a brand-new mouthguard. It's blood red and says FIGHTME on the front where my two new teeth are. I come to practice the next day, get down on my knees, slap myself across my face, and then put my little midget fists up. *Ready to rumble?* I shout through my mouth guard. Or rather: *Ruhee hoo rumhole.*

I make my stand.

No more pushups.

Except when Coach hears him call me a bitchass w-n-word.

No more ratting.

Except when Coach sees him throw elbows and knees and kicks at me and that one time he accidentally on purpose lets go of the rim with me lying on the ground and accidentally on purpose stomps me in the crotch so Coach goes and rats on him himself and TC has to come and apologize to me again.

Always: *My bad, dog. That ain't cool, man. I should know better, yo. Won't happen again, B.* And a fistbump.

He accidentally-on-purpose knees me in the nards setting a screen on me and I'm down on the ground wheezing for like five minutes so we have to end the drill early so I can ice my nuts.

My bad, dog. That ain't cool, man. I should know better, yo. Won't happen again, B. Fistbump.

He ball fakes me in the post, shakes me, pulls out the chair with me, leaves me to do a header, then stomps on my ass and leaves a big Jumpman Jordan footprint on his way to dunking on me and hanging on the rim and grabbing his junk and then pointing at me and laughing so loud the whole team starts laughing two as I stumble to get up and pull my shorts up?

My bad, dog…, etc. etc. **Fistbump.**

And the whole time him thinking I don't relish every minute of this.

This, my *White Man Can't Jump* moment. My own personal *Above the Rim*, my *He Got Game*, my *Hoop Dreams*.

TC's everything I'm not. Talented. Tall. Strong. Quick. Coordinated. Athletic. Good at basketball. Black. Talented. Tall. Strong. Quick. Not white. Not a wannabe. Not a w-n-word. Not suicidal. Not me.

Me:

That all you got, kid?

You gonna have to hit me harder than that, son.

Oh yeah, that feels good, Terrence. Keep on givin it to me like that.

This'd my moment to shine.

My moment to be Rudy.

My moment to be Mickey to his Rocky.

Does he slowly gain respect for me every time I got back up and came at him again?

Does he have pity on me for how pathetic I am as a no-talent scrub, practice-team, team manager, wannabe coach who can't even win a rebounding drill with a blocking pad?

Does he dismiss my entire existence as just some spare tire to jump through on the way to 20 more tires? As a human sweat stain to step around?

Do I sometimes consider killing myself because I am so pathetic and my whole life I've dreamed of playing college basketball against somebody like TC and this is the closest I'm ever going to get and the closest I'm getting is acting like a big dick with a lot of floor burns, a broken nose, two fake teeth, a sore bum, bum nards, and so many homophobic taunts for my troubles?

Does it hurt my feelings and question my role on the team when heading into our two biggest games of the season against first place UW-Stevens Point and second place UW-Platteville and I make the mistake of stripping TC of the ball on his way to dunking on me during the game walk-through and me getting too into toughening up and telling TC, *Who's your daddy now, TC?* which forces TC to haul off and deck me in front of the whole team, open up a gash four inches long, 40 stitches worth beside my right eye, which forces Coach to suspend TC for both games which then forces us to lose both games which forces us under .500 after we'd just gotten to .500 the first time in Coach's career which then forces the rest of the guys on the team to blame me and start calling me a bitchass f-g-word or f-g-word'y w-n-word, mostly under their breath when Coach isn't around and especially during practice drills where they all take it upon themselves to elbow me, knee me, and kick me in the junk any chance they get when Coach isn't looking?

All this and does it break my spirit? Make me question my miserable existence and the years and years and hours and hours of playing basketball and practicing basketball and living for nothing at all but basketball?

Maybe. A little.

But as Michael Jordan once said in a Nike commercial: *I've failed over and over and over again in my life. And that is why I succeed.*

As Martin Luther King Jr once said before he was assassinated for being a black man with opinions: *The ultimate measure of a man is not where he stands in moments of convenience and comfort, but where he stands at times of challenge and controversy.*

As Tupac once said in a song before he was assassinated for being a black man from the west coast with opinions about other black men from the east coast: *Gotta keep your head up.*

75

Because after all I have one job. To toughen TC up, to equal his dickishness, which also means toughening up and being a dick to the other guys up.

And because sometimes you have to take one step back as a dick to take two steps forward as a dick.

Like how probably nobody else realizes it but me, how despite the two losses, my getting punched by TC actually pulls the team together in their hatred of me for getting TC suspended. How I actually get the team to around TC in their desire to be a dick to me.

Does anybody show their appreciation after that two-game suspension/losing streak eventually leads to a three-game winning streak and back above .500?

No. No they don't.

But that's okay.

I am not in this to be liked. I am in this to make us all better.

By being the bigger dick.

But alas the road to being the biggest dick can be long and hard and full of twists and turns.

As in the very next week in rebounding drills when TC dunks it on me as usual but then tries to land on top of me again, yet instead of stomping my butt, I've rolled over such that he ends up stomping my face, which is sweaty and greasy, which causes him to roll his ankle on the way back down to earth.

Letting out a primal scream, a declaration of blame: *You little dumbass motherfuckin cocksuckin bitchass pussy!*

And Coach, with his first chance of finishing .500 on the line, at last losing his temper with me, letting out his own primal declaration of blame. *What the fuck were you thinking, Ben?* And: *You had one goddamn job, Drevlow.* And: *Are you trying to ruin this fucking season for me?*

Which I am ashamed to say, what finally breaks me. What finally forces me to start to sniveling and then shedding some tears even and quivering a little in my voice about how none of this is my fault, how I'm just trying to toughen him up and all I'm trying to do is make him better and how nobody even respects everything I do around here to bring all you fucking guys together and prepare y'all motherfuckers for greatness!

My own primal scream of me not taking the blame. My declaration of being pushed too damn far.

Which by then nobody is really listening to because they're forced to listen to TC screaming *cocksuckin, motherfuckin, little bitchass...* as he hammer-punches the sides of his stretcher as the trainers carry him off the court.

Which strikes me as a little soft and overly melodramatic— a stretcher for a guy who's just rolled his ankle? *Suck it up, buttercup,* that's what my dad'd've told me if I was trying to get out of doing chores.

Why don't you pull up your big boy pants and walk it off.

Ooh waah, does your whittle ankle hurt, Princess? Well now your whole body's gonna hurt because you owe me 20 suicides.

The things we say to young men to toughen them up instead of lifting them up with us.

The things that Coach himself would've been telling TC if he weren't the six-six athletic freak son of a two-time NBA all-star and this wasn't Coach's best chance to finish above .500 for the first time his career, first time in the history of the basketball program.

The things I'd've been telling TC myself if my heart hadn't just been broken.

What I tell Coach is I'm done. I don't belong on this team anymore. I am a distraction. I am worse than a distraction. I am a liability.

I have no business being on the floor with a guy like Terry Cummings Jr., I tell him. Even as a practice scrub/ball boy/equipment manager/statistician/wannabe assistant coach.

This is me falling on my sword. Taking one for the team. Falling on the grenade. To hopefully get out of the way and let them heal in time to maybe make a run for the playoffs.

So that's it? You have one accident? Get kicked in the face? Roll a guy's ankle a little? And that's it, you quit?

This is Coach talking, not me.

I give you a little talking to? Try to light a fire under your ass? You get some naughty words thrown your way? That's it? You can't hack it anymore?

Because TC's a dick to you? Because I'm a dick to you? Because the whole team is a dick to you?

After everything you've put up with? Everything Terrance has thrown at you? You know how many times TC has cursed out his coaches? His teammates? Anybody who gets in his way?

Because Terrance rolls his little ankle once and throws a fit? You're gonna let him be the bigger dick? The way he's always been the bigger dick?

And watch him quit when he can't get his way after this, watch him blame his ankle, blame you, blame me, blame his dad. When he's finally out on his ass because he can't blame nobody else but himself.

And I thought I really had somebody who was willing to stand up to him. Make a man out of him. Teach him what mental toughness really means.

And just when we need you to step up the most. Because it's next man up! It's always next man up.

And this is when you're going to tuck your tail between your hindlegs and run home crying?

Is that how I've coached you? Is that how I've mentored you? Is that the model I've put out for you?

Coach flat out calling me out. Saying something to that effect. Give or take.

Which forces me to start crying again. Which I'm not proud of but goddamn it I'm only a man and sometimes men cry—especially men who are practice scrubs/ball boys/equipment managers/wannabe assistant coaches.

So you gonna quit on me, Drevlow?

No, I say crying.

No what?

No I guess not, I say crying.

I guess not?

I'm not gonna quit, I say trying to cry less.

Let me hear you mean it.

I ain't gonna quit on you, Coach, I say. I ain't gonna quit on the team, I say. I ain't quitting on that fucking dick either!

Or something like that.

The whole thing pretty emotional.

Like the way nobody'd ever actually cared one way or the other before. At least no man. Not my dad. Definitely not my brother.

This, this is why I have to come back. Why I have to be there TC whether he hates me or not. To kick him in the ass.

Or to let him kick me in the ass and me not complain about it.

So I don't go drive myself off a bridge. I don't go home and chase a fifth of Hennessy with a bottle of Drano. I don't get drunk and come back to the locker room and hang myself by TC's shoestrings in TC's locker and leave a note saying, *I hope you feel good about yourself now —signed B (aka your bitchass w-n-word).*

I come back and I kick TC's ass. I become his own personal trainer. Watch him do his rehab exercises. Call him a pussy when he complains. Ask him if he wants to call home to daddy. Ask him if he wants to quit and go work at the 7-Eleven.

If this is a dick contest, I'm a regular Ron Jeremy.

He calls me a bitchass w-n-word.

I'm like Jay-Z, I'm gettin that dirt off my shoulders.
He calls me a little f-g-word'y scrubbyass cocksucker.
I'm like Taylor Swift, I'm shaking it off.
Until…

Two weeks later and TC is back on the court.

One week left of the season.

Two games to get over .500 and make the playoffs.

Who's the bitchass w-n-word, now, eh?

I don't say that.

Though imagine how cool it'd've been if I had.

Who's the bitchass w-n-word, now, TC?

Who's the bitchass w-n-word, now, every other guy on the team who's been motherfuckin me under their breath ever since TC rolled his ankle on my face?

But I don't say any of that.

Which is to say I let my balling say it for me.

We're doing rebounding drills.

Except instead of being down in the trenches and beating on TC with the blocking pad and potentially re-injuring his ankle, I'm out on the three-point line letting them fly.

All this time and I've never really unveiled my hidden weapon on TC.

My three-ball.

The way my dad taught me how to shoot like Larry Bird when I was a kid. How I wanted nothing more than to shoot jumpers like Michael fucking Air Jordan, and my dad was having none of it.

Nice little set shots, but from over my shoulder. Like the whitest honky to ever play the game.

Get it up there, he'd say. Let 'er fly. Skim the sky.

And if I didn't, if I stubbornly refused to not shoot like I thought Michael Jordan shot, he'd just reach over and swat it.

My dad no two-time NBA All-Star but he was six-three, former Minnesota State High School champion.

Me 12 years old, like five-six.
Get it up there!
Swat.
Me 13 years old, like five-seven.
Really cock 'er back.
Swat.
Me 14 years old, like five-nine.
Are you never gonna learn?
Swat.
Me 14 years old, like five-nine.
You ain't no Mike Jordan.
Swat.
Me 15 years old, like five-ten.
I hate to tell you this, but you ain't black, son.
Swat.
Me 16 years old, like five eleven.
If you aren't gonna listen, what's the point of me even tryin with you?
Swat.
Me 17 years old, five eleven (my dad having hunched over to maybe six-one, six two at best).
You might as well duck and chuck it, the way you refuse to try it my way.
So I do it. I duck and chuck.
Unleash a rainbow.
I don't see it go in.
I can't see it over my dad's reach.
But I hear the bank.
And then the woosh.
And then I'm 18, still five eleven, maybe five eleven and a half.
Grip it and rip it, my dad says.
I don't. I duck and chuck it.
All I hear is the swish.

I'm supposed to be missing. That's the whole point. I'm supposed to miss the three so TC and the rest of them can contest the shot and go rebound.

It's supposed to be half-speed. Not much more than a walk-through. Just working on the mechanics. Nobody getting hurt.

And I'm not trying to be a hero.

I'm just ducking and chucking, trying to miss pretty. Make the ball go straight up off the back rim.

It's just that I bank in the first one. Without calling it.

Then I go and bank another one, not even trying to miss pretty, just miss. I'm not even looking. I'm looking at TC to see if he's going through the footwork right.

I hear the bank and then the swish.

Coach says, You know, this ain't the Drevlow show, right?

Guys chuckle a little bit.

TC switches off the guy guarding me. Gets up in me a bit. Calls me w-n-word trash under his breath.

I have to take two dribbles back just to get a shot off with TC's seven-foot wingspan in my face.

This time no bank. It's way downtown bang.

Coach shakes his head. The rest of the guys shake their head.

How about we try to get a rebound, eh? Coach says to me.

TC telling me to pull another one out of my bitchass drawers.

So I miss a few. Miss bad. Line drive ricochets. One that just hits the top of the backboard and caroms all the way back to Coach.

Who just looks at me.

Looks at me like can't you even do this? I gave you that big pep talk for this?

Or something like that.

I take my time with the next one. Imagine Larry looping one up there higher than the backboard even.

I let 'er fly. Watch 'er scrape the sky.

Shit, TC says.

Nothing but net.

Same thing the next time.

Shit. Swish.

TC's up in my grill, I can smell his breath. It doesn't smell good.

If I were to look up, I'd see that nobody else is going through the motions. Not even Coach. They've just smiling and shaking their heads.

But I'm not looking. I've got my head down. My eyes focused on TC's numbers. 2-3. As in: Michael James Jordan. As in: my old number from high school.

There's no halfassing it now. This is nothing bull fullassing. Fullassing, dicks swinging.

I take two dribbles back, head fake, watch TC go flying, take one dribble back, set my feet, duck and chuck. Nothin but net.

Coach is full on laughing now. Having never laughed before, it's a little disturbing.

Somebody asks if TC wants his jock back.

Somebody else asks if TC's gon take that shit from B, yo.

B being me.

No longer bitchass. Just B.

Don't you go be breakin TC's ankles again, you hear, B?

TC takes the ball and shoves it into my gut.

I can't help it, a little smirk creeps over my face.

TC gets down and squeaks his feet, slaps the court with both hands, which to be honest is a real white-boy thing to do. Like Duke-Bobby-Hurly thing to do.

Watch out, you don't hurt yourself, I say.

He doesn't say nothing.

I turn my back to him, start dribbling like I'm gonna back him down, big-brother style, big-daddy style.

I don't say midget on my back. But I want to. The way I want to teach him a lesson finally. A lesson about mental toughness versus physical toughness.

Dribble, dribble, step back, spin, head fake. Watch TC go flying by once more. Set my feet. Let 'er rain.

Somebody yells, Yeah B.

Somebody else yells, In yo face, T.

Coach says, All right all right. Last one.

Coach says, Winner does laundry. He winks at me.

TC calls for the ball. He says, man gimme that ball. He slaps the ball with one hand and then the other. He grabs the ball with both hands and squeezes it like to pop it. Hits his own head with it twice.

Then he simply sets it on the court in front of me as if to say checkmate.

Or: Try that shit one more time, bitch.

But it's not bitchass. It's not the w-n-word or the f-g-word. Just bitch.

Everybody has cleared out of the way.

Everybody is watching, looking at each other, then back at us.

What a silly thing to watch, they must be thinking. This little practice-team scrub/ball boy/equipment manager/wannabe assistant coach/bitchass w-n-word.

And Terry Cummings Junior.

What a joke it must be to all of them, even Coach. Everybody but me and TC.

I pick up the ball. Flip it from hand to hand.

Fake it like I'm gonna throw it in his face. That old big-brother move, that old-man move, that big-dick move.

He doesn't flinch.

He doesn't take his eyes off my numbers. Practice jersey 6-9.

Another kind of joke. A number so big I couldn't even play in a game because the ref couldn't spell out my number with two hands.

He's got one hand hand-checking my hip, the other slapping at the ball.

From a distance it must look like I'm being swallowed up by another man's shadow, a much bigger man's shadow trying to take me whole.

Somebody yells, Rip his shit, T.

Somebody else yells, Take his shit, B.

I turn my back, do a little Jordan shimmy, follow that up with a Dream shake, come back with a jab step, head fake.

He takes two steps back and nearly loses his balance with his wrapped-up ankle getting in the way.

I've never felt this strong before. I'm ready for an arm-wrestling tournament if that's what it would take to teach TC his lesson.

Growing up my dad used to call me a mental midget for how stubborn I was to not listen to him. He'd say, Boy, I don't care how tall you grow or how many weights you lift, you'll always be a mental midget if you never learn to listen.

I imagine TC's dad telling him the same thing. And I imagine him saying the same thing again with every time he got kicked out of a different college.

It's sad the little things that stand between some people and being brothers.

Where's your daddy now, bitch?

I don't feel good about saying it. I don't want to say it. If I weren't completely in the zone, I'd probably feel sick to my stomach saying it.

If I didn't have to say it…

I whisper it under my breath so only he can hear it.

Where's your daddy now…, bitch?

Which is my moment. My move before my move. My mental move. I maybe five eleven and a half but I'll be a mental midget no more.

I do a double head fake, a shot fake upon another shot fake. Make like I'm gonna do a fade-away, Larry Legend style from long range.

Even lift one knee up to get him.

And I get him.

Man it's almost sad the way I get him.

Like meeting your hero and seeing him too drunk to sign an autograph.

Watch him fly by.

Take one dribble to set my feet.

I go ahead and do a little shimmy with my hips and look over my shoulder but don't really look over my shoulder.

Just for show.

For the lesson.

I cock it back like one of them old timey catapults.

I grip it and rip it.

I duck and chuck.

I'm not even looking.

Which is lucky.

I don't have to see TC come flying back in from behind.

I don't have to see the ball go flying backwards.

I don't have see the tip of his elbow come crashing down on my eyeball.

It's all darkness and feeling like I've just been shot.

In the eye.

Somebody's yelling, Damn!

Somebody else is yelling, Yeah, T!

Somebody else is yelling, Oh shit.

I'm not yelling anything.

I'm not even cursing in my head.

I'm flat on my back and feeling TC's body draped over mine.

I can smell his deodorant starting to fail.

I can hear his heavy breathing in my ear, I can feel it.

I can feel the blood pooling in my eye socket.

Oh shit, somebody says. Oh fuck.

It's TC.

Do I have an eyeball anymore? Am I going to be a pirate for the rest of my life? I had a kid in high school with a glass eye. His name was Nelson. We all called him One-Eyed Nelly. I called him that.

Was this my karma?

What would they call me now? Black Beard Ben? Patch Drevlow?

Dawg, I can hear TC saying as he does a push up off me. Damn.

I can hear somebody else whisper, Where's with dude's eyeball, yo?

I can hear TC say shut the fuck up, yo.

I can hear Coach tell somebody to go get a trainer.

I can hear Coach tell somebody else to go call 911.

I can hear TC tell me his bad. Tell me his fault. Tell me he fucked up. I can feel him grab my hand and fistbump it. You're gonna be straight dude. You straight, dawg. You gonna be straight, B.

I'm thinking about that scene in *Any Given Sunday* when dude's eyeball is just lying there out on the turf.

I'm thinking of Nelly's glass eye would never look the same direction as his good eye.

I'm thinking about guys like TC trash-talking after they'd hit threes. That's in your eye, they'd say and then put up three fingers and make a monocle with their thumb and pointer finger.

It's all in the eye of the beholder, I think. I almost want to giggle.

I can hear TC telling guys to get out of the way. Give him some space, yo.

You straight, B? somebody asks.

Yo, B gonna be straight. Don't even ask that, n-word. Why you even ask that, n-word?

I can hear trainers coming in and kneeling next to me and whispering things to each other and then asking me if I can feel this limb and that limb, this toe and that finger.

I can.

I can feel everything.

Everything except my eye.

Hey yo, I just got the killer eye, I want to say. I don't.

I say, yes sir and no sir and yes sir and no sir and no sir.

I don't ask if they've found my eye yet.

I don't dare open my good eye.

They're carting me off the court now for some reason.

They've wrapped my head like a mummy and they're carting me off and all I can think to do is give a thumbs up, like those guys in the NFL when they've broken their necks or backs or are barely conscious.

A few guys clap.

This is all silly. I know that even as they are carting me off with my face wrapped like a mummy. I know that without even opening my good eye to know I can still see at all.

This is me in my defining moment as a basketball player. I drained six three's on Terry Cumming's kid and then he rejected my shit like shit's never been rejected.

And just for good measure, he took my eye, my shooter's eye, from me.

This is all so silly, I'd be giggling if I weren't feeling sick from all the blood pulling around my eye socket.

Where's my eyeball? I want to say. Where's my trophy? My memorabilia?

Is TC crying? For joy or for guilt or for victory? The big game is tomorrow. Will he use this experience to motivate him?

This is for B's eyeball, yo, he'll say in the huddle before they go onto the court.

It's so silly how proud I am of myself at this moment. It's so silly the things we take pride in as men. The things that we use to define ourselves. The things we use to separate ourselves from others, the rest of the wolf pack.

It's so silly how profound I'm trying to be.

I'm a mummy with no eye. I'm perfectly capable of walking like a mummy of putting away all the basketballs like a mummy. Doing the laundry like a mummy. Getting all the uniforms ready to go on the road.

How many eyes do you need to record the game on the video camera? The answer is one.

How many eyes do you need to make Gatorade from powder and fill up a five-gallon cooler? The answer is one.

It's so silly.

So silly how humiliated I am when the EMT unwraps the gauze off my head, peels off the dried blood, and says, Oh, nice, oh yeah. It's still there, buddy.

How soft am I? How weak? How bitchass can a man be? How much of a mental midget must I be to get so caught up as the hero with one eye?

Do I have the power to win the big game for us with one eye and one other eye? Does double-vision motivate anyone to achieve new athletic heights? How about a measly 12 stitches?

I don't.

It doesn't.

They don't.

TC breaks his shooting hand punching his locker the next game. He fractures the bones for real. Fucks up his ligaments.

We lose.

We lose again.

Why bother even trying at that point? Who has it worse? The guy with double vision and a few stitches or the guy that's probably ended his college career turning his anger back on himself.

There's a lesson here somewhere.

A hard-fought friendship, hard-won respect, it's worth more than a below 500 win-loss record, more than a stupid play-off game.

The things that men have to overcome to learn to see each other.

I wish I could say these things and I wish they could be true.

I wish I could say that TC and I learned these lessons, having toughened each other up.

I wish I could say at the very least TC's dad showed up to watch him learn.

I wish I could've introduced him to my dad and say how many times my dad had made me watch you guard Larry Bird and get schooled night in night out.

I haven't spoken to TC in 20 years. I used to keep track of him best I could, see his name on some internet article about a European team. That quick stint he had with the G-League.

The last thing he said to me—or at least the last thing I can remember him saying to me—Man, 12 stitches. 12 fucking stitches? Going out in a stretcher. Fucking with everybody's head like that. The day before a game? Man, that's some weakass shit. That's some bitchass f-g-word'y w-n-word stuff. How you even gonna show up to the most important game of the year after all that with 12 fucking stitches? Shit, man.

The last thing I said to him—I think—maybe something like *My bad, dawg. That ain't cool, man. Won't happen again, T.* And a fistbump left hanging. An unrequited fistbump.

Does TC even remember any of all that? What we learned, what we didn't?

That one moment before all that where he felt guilty enough about thinking he'd knocked my eyeball out that he wanted to protect me from everything around me.

How long he laid there on top of me after he thought he'd knocked my eye out.

I don't imagine he does.

I can't imagine I would if I were in his shoes—his size-15 retro Jordans.

But sometimes I like to think it'd've all been worth it. One eyeball, for one moment of real kinship between Terry Cumming's kid and the bitchass w-n-word from Northernass Wisconsin.

How everything might've gone after that if only I'd become a pirate.

How maybe we could've made both our fathers proud of us, an eye for an eye.

It's just sad. So sad and so silly.

One big joke.

We laugh so we cry so we don't die of shame, alone, bastards and orphans and bitchass big sad swinging dicks.

DEPUTY SCOTTY

I'VE MADE THE MISTAKE OF COMING BACK HOME.
I'm doing 35 in a 25 after bar close.

In Northernass Wisconsin, it's illegal for cops to set up shop outside of bars and pull everybody over.

But that doesn't mean they can't park their cars two blocks down on either side of the two town bars, one of them being a bowling alley called The Super Bowl.

I've never been pulled over before.

This is a new thing for me, drinking and driving.

I've spent my whole high school and college career telling myself that drinking would stop me from accomplishing my dream of playing college basketball.

Now that I've graduated and my college basketball career never amounted to anything other than being a practice team scrub/team manager, I am ready to begin my post-basketball career of getting drunk and trying to forget all the time I spent not drinking only to end up where I've ended up.

I'm driving my Bronco II, which is what all the druggies drive from my hometown.

I got a deal on it. Which is to say, my dad got a deal on it because it was totaled. They're top heavy and too many druggies think they look cool whipping shitties out on the dirt roads or going muddin out in the boonies.

I was never a druggie but I am now drunk.

My glove compartment is packed with candy bar wrappers, Hardee's burger wrappers, and Mike & Ike's having spilled out long ago and I never cleaned up.

I'm rustling through it to find my registration. Honestly, I'm not sure what the registration even looks like. My dad is the one who applied for it and put it in my glove compartment and all I know is that I need it.

In high school, I was a teacher's aide for the Driver's Ed instructor who was also the gym teacher who was also the girls basketball coach.

Her name was Shari.

I had two female gym teachers in high school. Both of them named Shari (or Sherry). Both of them coached girls' basketball.

There was hot Sherry and scary Shari.

My Driver's Ed teacher was scary Shari and she took over coaching for hot Sherry after she came out as a lesbian and a bunch of homophobic parents got her fired for supposedly looking at the girls naked and talking to them inappropriately when they were naked.

I guess they were less scared of scary Shari looking at their daughters naked than they were hot Sherry, which seems both wrong and misguided but also on brand for Northernass Wisconsin.

If they fired a coach every time he/she/they talked to their players inappropriately when they were naked, every coach I had—including my sixth-grade coach—would've gotten fired. Some of them justifiably so. For reasons having nothing to do with homosexuality.

But that's not the point.

My point is that I know what the legal alcohol limit is for a guy my height and weight and I know I'm past it and I know what the fine and punishment is for a DUI (or a dewey as we called them).

Remain calm, I remind myself.

Retrieve your registration where you have stowed it for easy retrieval in case of a routine traffic stop.

Wait for the officer to walk up to your driver's side and ask you to roll down your window.

My window is electric and broken and doesn't roll down is my first problem. I've got a wooden door jammed down there to keep the window from falling. This is the extent of my knowledge of car repair.

My second problem is that the cop pulling me over is Scotty Sanderson, aka the guy who used to be the assistant coach on my sixth-grade basketball team.

His dad, Scott Sanderson Sr, the chief of police, being my head sixth-grade coach.

His youngest son, Stevie Sanders, my same age, having been the starting point guard, me his backup.

In my less mature years, I may have let it be known not so subtly that the only reason Stevie started over me was because he was not only the coach's kid, but the police chief's kid. My evidence being the myriad reasons that I was far superior and more than happy to recite.

The least of which was Stevie along with his brother Scotty Junior and his dad Scott Senior knew as much about as much about basketball as I knew about fixing up totaled Broncos.

This was strictly a volunteer gig for dad to bond with his sons when he wasn't hard at work giving people speeding tickets, DUIs, and giving school talks about the importance of driving safety and saying no to drugs and alcohol.

Whoa whoa whoa, Deputy Scott Sanderson Jr. says when I go to open my door instead of rolling down my window.

He has one hand on his gun at his side and the other hand on the flashlight blinding my eyes.

Of course right now I don't know that he is my former sixth-grade assistant basketball coach.

I say, Sorry officer and hold up my hands like he might shoot me. I say that my window doesn't roll down.

He says, Do you even know what I could've done to you right then?

I say, Sorry officer. I wasn't thinking.

He is still shining his flashlight in my face.

I am focusing on my S's and sounding not drunk. *Sorry officer* is a surprisingly tricky one-two combo when you're pulled over drunk.

With the flashlight on me and all the hullabaloo about not getting shot, I still don't recognize him. Also he looks to weigh about 200 pounds past his coaching days. (He never even actually played basketball in high school, neither did Stevie).

Or maybe I didn't catch his name when he walked up to my car.

License and registration, sir.

I'm not *not* feeling like I'm going to spew and so maybe I reach for my glove box a little too assertively. The passenger side floormat is already covered with empty bottles of Mountain Dew and Red Bull. And so add to that about five different boxes of candy and candy bar wrappers and a couple wrenches and the Leatherman my dad gave me fall out, which I then remember, has a knife on it, which I am now fixating on.

Frick frick frick frick frick, I'm thinking as I fixate on the knife on the Leatherman I never use.

Whoa whoa whoa, he says. Are you trying to get yourself shot?

He has his hand on his holster again. I'm looking at his holster to avoid looking into the blinding flashlight. Also because I don't want to look at the passenger side seat Leatherman with the knife on it and because I don't want to be shot.

I say sorry officer. I was looking for my registration.

Registration is also a hard word to not sound drunk on.

Deputy Scott Sanderson Jr. says, What are you thinking? You could be pulling out a gun for all I know. Do you want to get shot?

I have my hands up again. Not wanting to get shot.

My hometown is 1400 people on the shore of Lake Superior in Northernass Wisconsin, where the biggest crime is driving drunk—driving drunk on snowmobiles, driving drunk on four-wheelers, driving drunk on tractors, driving drunk on riding lawnmowers, driving drunk on bicycles, motorcycles, driving drunk on ice, driving drunk through small ponds, streams, and mud bogs.

And teenagers smoking weed while being drunk underaged.

I'm just driving drunk.

But I have seen the cop shows, not the least of which being *COPS*.

As already established: I am not black.

But I do have a shaved head, a House of Pain goatee and six different scars from six different sets of stitches from playing basketball as a scrappy little wannabe black guy white boy guarding bigger guys too up close and personal and getting elbowed and *accidentally* punched in the face on a semi-regular basis.

And for sometimes making it not so subtly known that I could out hustle anybody who wanted to step to this (at least before I got to college and half the team was black and six inches taller than I was and could dunk on my head).

Basically I was the Rudy Ruettiger of basketball players.

And much like Rudy Ruettiger, where I grew up where everybody was as white as they come (except of course for Boykin the one black kid who could never keep his grades up to make the team anyway).

So it's the skinhead/meth-head-looking punks who get profiled.

And let it be said: I am neither a neo-nazi skinhead nor a meth-head.

I did however grow up listening to Tupac and idolizing Jordan and trying to look like my favorite black rappers/basketball players.

In Northernass Wisconsin they have a word for wannabes like me. It starts with a *W* and rhymes with *trigger*.

And even with the *W*, it's not a word that white guys would actually say out loud if there were other actual black guys around to put them in their places.

Even back in sixth grade, older guys in high school like Scotty Sanders Jr. would call me a little *w-n-word* with my baggy shorts hanging down my ass and my two-sizes too big retro North Carolina Jordan jersey, and my retro Jordan high-tops and black Nike socks, and bright white Nike headband and matching armbands.

Why don't you work on the fundamentals like passing and setting picks and being a good teammate instead of acting like such a little w-n-word all the time, Scotty used to tell me when I would make it known that I felt that I was three-times the player that his little brother was who never passed and never set a pick and was generally dumber than Lonny our school janitor with severe brain damage.

Now let's try this again nice and easy. License and registration.

I ask him if it's okay now to reach down and find my registration on the floor mat with all the Mountain Dew bottles and Red Bull cans, candy wrappers, Hardee's Hot Ham and Cheese wrappers, and Mike and Ike's.

He says, Slowly.

I ask him if it is okay to reach down into my pockets and grab my wallet with my license in it.

He says, Slowly.

This is when I realize it's Scotty Sanderson Jr. my former sixth-grade assistant basketball coach.

He says, Jesus fuckin Christ, it's Benny fuckin Drevlow, you little fuckin *w-n-word*.

He's flashing the flashlight from my license to my face.

You probably don't even remember me, do you, you little college boy Mr. Bigtime *w-n-word*?

Hey... Coach... I say holding my hand up to shade my eyes. You a deputy now, I see.

Benny fuckin Drevlow, he says again while he leans in my open door and shines around the interior. Sniffing, sniffing.

I thought I'd never see the day, he says still shining his flashlight around my interior, sniffing sniffing.

Mister Straight and Narrow. Mister No Fun Basketball Boy. Mister Wannabe N-word, himself. As I live and breathe.

How's your dad doin? I say trying not to sound drunk. He still chiefin?

Hell nah, the old man's too old for this shit. Him and my stepmom bought an RV and retired to Jacksonville. It's Florida but with none of the n-words or s-p-words rhyming with *hicks*.

Old Stevey? He on the force, too?

Hell nah. That dumb fuck's too stupid to pass the exam. He runs pull tabs at the Super Bowl on weekends and works nights scrubbing toilets at the school.

With Lonny?

Y'up.

I say that's cool before I realize that it's not cool and hope that Scotty doesn't think I'm being condescending to his brother the janitor/pull-tabs operator.

Benny fuckin goddamn Drevlow.

He's looking at my license some more. Looking at my registration.

You know why pulled you over, Benny fuckin Drevlow?

It's one of those trick questions.

I say, nah, sorry Scotty.

Sorry *Deputy* Sanderson, he corrects me.

You know how fast you were goin?

I say, nah, sorry. I start to say *Scotty* but catch myself and turn it into *Sir*.

Thirty-fuckin-eight, dickhead.

I say sorry, but this time leave it at that. I'm trying to look him in the face to make it seem like I'm not hiding anything but the flashlight is making me dizzy and then when I look in my rearview to avoid looking at the flashlight, the cherries make me even dizzier.

I suppose you've forgotten what the speed limit is, Mr. Bigtime College Boy.

I have forgotten the speed limit. Which I really shouldn't have with all my time grading Driver's Ed tests in the back of the Driver's Ed car.

Twenty-fuckin five, Benny Drevlow. Twenty-fuckin-five.

I'm not entirely sure how to respond to this information without pissing him off more: *Oh shit, I'm sorry. Oh damn, I totally didn't realize that. Oh fuck, man, that was totally reckless of me to be driving like that.*

Like what?

Like drunk. And fast.

I don't say any of that.

I say, Really?

He says, Really, fuckhead.

I say, Damn.

He says, Damn right, dickhead.

He says, This is what you do, huh?

He says, You come slummin back home with her dick between your legs and suddenly you're too good to drive the speed limit.

Or stay under the legal limits for drinking and driving?

He doesn't say it. I don't say it.

My door is still open and occasionally a car'll have to swerve by to miss us and Scotty will say watch where you're going fucknuts.

I keep wrinkling up my nose and trying to see if I can smell alcohol on my breath while simultaneously trying not to get caught smelling if I have alcohol on my breath.

Nah man, I say.

Nah *Deputy*, he says.

Nah *Deputy*, I say. It's not like that at all. I ain't no big-time college boy? Do I look like I'm some big-time college boy?

My big-time college moment? I once made six straight threes in a practice drill against the best player on the team, this six-six black guy whose dad was a two-time all-star for the Milwaukee Bucks.

On my seventh attempt, he swatted my shit all the way down to the other basket, hollered get that shit out of here, *w-n-word,* and came down with his elbow on my eyeball.

I got 12 stitches and I still saw double for two weeks. Still see double from time to time, especially if I've been drinking.

Like tonight.

Scottie, after what seems like an hour, finally waddles back to his cop car to fill out some paperwork and to check if I'm a known drug dealer or child molester.

I practice reciting the alphabet backwards. Z-Y-X... is as far as I get before I have to start reciting forwards. I practice touching my nose with my eyes closed.

I sniff sniff sniff my breath. I look in the rearview and blink to see if they look too bloodshot. I move my finger from side to side to see my eyes to see if they track.

I think about my year of sixth-grade basketball with Coach Chief Sanderson and Assistant Coach Scotty Jr. How I only started one game the whole season, the championship game, a game I never actually played in.

The week my oldest brother killed himself. His wake on Saturday of the big game. I think about Coach coming to the house the night he killed himself and asking me all these questions and me thinking my brother had been murdered or something when it was just that he killed himself.

Did somebody murder my brother? I blurted out at some point during his questioning me—12-year-old me.

Oh no, son. No, nobody came and hurt your brother but himself. This is just what I have to do.

This is what my basketball coach has to do. Grill me on what happened to my brother. This is the first time I ever realize that Coach has to do things as police chief other than coming to our classes to tell us about saying no to drugs and alcohol.

I remember that what finally breaks me that night is not the questions about my dead brother. It's the answer to me asking Coach if I was going to be able to play in the championship that weekend.

Oh no, son. Don't you worry about that. You just worry about your family right now. That's your role you have to step up and play, being there for your family. Your real team.

And yet I ended up scoring 21 points in that game. Got my name in the paper: *Dribble scores 21 to win the 1990-91 sixth-grade city championship.*

The only time I ever got my name in the paper: *Dribble.*

A town of 1400 people and they get my name wrong. My one moment to shine.

Of course it'd been Stevie anyway. Coach making him wear my jersey 23 in honor of me not being able to be there because my brother had killed himself and I had to go to the wake even though I'd've much rather played in the championship.

Stevie scoring out of his ass and passing even less than usual. All in honor of me.

Coach cutting that story out of the paper and giving it to me along with the actual trophy at the funeral the next day. Me getting a trophy at my own brother's funeral.

Who gets a trophy at a funeral?

I did.

Why Coach would even show up in the first place? It's not like he had solved the big murder or anything. It's not like he was a close family friend. He was a volunteer sixth-grade basketball coach who always started his shitty son over me just because he wanted to make Stevie forget about all the nights his dad never came home.

I'm chewing on stale Mike & Ikes, thinking that might help with a breathalyzer, when Scotty comes back knocking on my window that doesn't work.

I do a full spit take and send them flying. I'm literally on a cop show right now. I'm the butt of the joke. The punk who needs to be taught a lesson.

He doesn't wait for me to open the door this time. Doesn't want any funny business. He yanks it open himself, no flashlight this time, just a pink piece of paper.

Benny, Benny, Benny, he says shaking his head as he hands me the ticket. I thought we taught you better than this.

Now take Stevie, he's an idiot. Couldn't pass the police entrance test after four attempts. Rides a bike to work now. Had to take that dumbass's license after like the fifth DUI. Not even Pops could save him from himself.

But you? You thought you were so much better, didn't you? Mr. Benny fucking Drevlow Big Time College Basketball W-N-Word.

And look where you are now?

Drunk?

I don't say that.

I just say, I know I know and shake my head looking at my hands on the steering wheel, the one slimy Mike and Ike I spit out on the dashboard.

What do you think my dad would say if he could see you like this?

I know, I say and shake my head again. Then I look up and look him in the eyes for the first time all night. No flashlight. Just those big beady eyes now sunken into his moon face. Fogged up glasses he never used to have to wear. A beard with the start of graying in it around his chin.

In sum: the spitting image of his old man, back when his old man was Coach.

I'm sorry, I say again. I don't know what I was thinking.

It's messed up, the way Scotty's fucking with me. Making me think I'm gettin a dewey for sure, then making me think I'm goin to get away with a speeding ticket, and me wondering if it's because he's just too bad at his job to realize what a fuckup drunk I'm becoming or if it's because he knows and he just doesn't want to bust my balls too hard.

Or maybe he just doesn't want to do the paperwork.

Or of course the obvious that I'm white and not black (not that there are any black people to pull over in this hick town).

But still, I'm having to now think about his old man and my dead brother and that goddamn trophy and my name spelled wrong in the paper.

Dribble scores 21 and leads the Castle Guards to victory in the city championship.

That's what our team's name was. The Castle Guards. Which really we were just the Knights, but somebody'd decided to call us the Castle Guards. As if we were all here to protect our home like a castle.

It didn't make sense to me then or now.

The Prison Guards is more like it, I used to joke.

Do you have even the first clue what it's like to be in prison, son? Coach scolded me one time.

I didn't say anything. I put my head down.

Well just you watch where you're heading with all this attitude, boy, and you might damn well find out.

Last thing Scottie says to me: Well go get yourself home safe, now, Benny fuckin Drevlow. And I don't wanna ever see your w-n-word ass like this again. Break my old man's goddamn heart if I were to tell him.

Then he goes ahead and slams the door on me. Waddles back. Turns off the cherries. And guns it off back down toward the bars. On the hunt for some other drunken driver acting like an asshole.

PART II.
SOUTHERNASS
GEORGIA

CLEM & MEL & MIKEY

WE'VE MOVED ON DOWN to Southernass Georgia for my future ex-wife's job and we're living next door to a Christ, Science church.

For the first few weeks, I've been confusing it with the Church of Scientology.

This is just one example of the type of stupidity people who get to know me have to put up with.

People like my future ex-wife.

I keep making jokes about Tom Cruise popping by for after-church barbecues.

And aliens coming to shoot us with their anxiety and depression laser guns.

This all should say something about my Wisconsin upbringing, the things I know about Scientology versus the Church of Christ, Scientist.

And the things I don't.

My future ex-wife has to explain again and again that it's Christ-*comma*-Scientist.

She says they believe in Christ the same Christian alien everybody does, not random psychologically traumatizing aliens come up with from science fiction writers and unhinged Hollywood celebrities.

I ask if that means Christian Scientists are actual scientists who happen to believe that Jesus was a scientist, like, in addition to being a carpenter and shepherd and father, son, and holy ghost.

She shoots me her look. Her look that means she isn't sure if I'm this dumb or if I'm this unfunny. I've come to know that look too well of late.

They're the type of Christian who think hospitals and modern medicine are the devil and Jesus saves all.

They should call it Jesus Christ, MD, I tell her.

She doesn't laugh.

The way she hasn't laughed at anything I've said since we moved down to Southernass Georgia.

If I were a better husband, I would be more emotionally attuned to this no-laughing look than I am.

I would be less fixated with the church next door.

Who am I to judge which aliens we should believe in and whether hospitals and doctors and psychiatry as a whole is necessary.

But then there's the homeless guys outside our window.

Who are all black.

Whereas my future-ex-wife and I are *all* white.

It's like that joke: *It might be tough right now, but if we stay together I think we're gonna be all white.*

My wife doesn't find my white-guilt jokes funny. She worries that one day I'm going to make a white-guilt joke to one of her colleagues and she might get canceled on my behalf.

I make jokes to deal with the awkwardness of our white guilt vis-a-vis all the black homeless guys sleeping under the church awning five feet outside our bedroom window.

I think I would feel less guilty if at least a couple of them were white.

Like I could still make an argument that homeless white people are still more privileged than homeless black people.

These are the thoughts I have when pulling out the trash and recycling.

Up north you could get five cents a can and ten cents a bottle, so I'd say Have at 'er boys, every time I'd bring out the recycling. Even though the homeless guys wouldn't show up until night.

Down here, you have to pay more to recycle, let alone cash incentives for cans or bottles.

I don't say have at 'er boys when I bring out the trash anymore.

I think to myself: How many times is enough times to give the guys 20 bucks?

What about leftovers? Is it offensive to bring them leftovers that would've been trashed anyway?

And should I be making a more concerted effort to eat leftovers in lieu of wasting them vis-a-vis There are a bunch of homeless guys right outside that would love to have these leftovers?

And then there's the heat and while it's not the cold we had up north, down here the heat's the heat and the humidity's the humidity and how can we feel good about ourselves sleeping with our central air on when they're out there sleeping with the gnats and mosquitoes and the humidity and the heat and the potential to get arrested and/or beaten to an inch of their life by their homeless peers and/or the very people who are supposed to protect them.

It's unclear if the homeless guys are believers in Christ-comma-Scientist or not.

I'm guessing not.

I've never seen any Christ-comma-Scientists give them any money or food.

And the way the Christ-comma-Scientists come and kick them out every couple days. Threaten to call the cops.

I'd probably be a lot less jokey about the Christ-comma-Scientists if they weren't kicking out the homeless guys every couple nights.

It's like that joke: *The economy might be shit right now, but have faith and the Christ, Scientists will be all white.*

But then it's not like I'm exactly Mr. White Savior either.

Sleeping every night with my central air and not asking them to come have dinner with us or if they want to have a beer on me or if I have any extra blankets they could use to soften the concrete awning they sleep on.

I must admit that I worry for my future ex-wife's safety (though I don't feel good about it). It can be quite confusing sometimes—deciding if you want to be the white savior or if you want to be the white knight of the patriarchy.

Do I know their names?

It's not like it's the same ones all the time. It's not like there is just some Greek Chorus of faceless homeless black guys.

Some have short beards, some have long. Some have winter hats, some have regular hat hats, a couple don't even have hats to protect them from the sun.

I think one of them is Clem. Another one is Mel. And then Mikey.

The fucked-up part is that I only know those because those are the ones who come up and ask if I need any yard work done and then I have to tell them no because if I'm not doing the yard work myself then I am not carrying my own weight as a future ex-husband.

It's one of those catch-22 deals.

I've paid Clem and Mel and Mikey each about 50 bucks over the course of five months.

It's a tricky thing.

Sometimes they come over and I'm not there to answer the door and they ask my future ex-wife if she needs any more yard work done.

And that fucks my thing up.

My thing being that my future ex-wife is basically my sugar mama.

But a sugar momma who expects me to at least help out around the house.

Walk the dogs. Clean the house. Make dinner. Do the yard.

All of which I have no problem with as a man.

I don't believe in pants or no pants in a marriage.

I'm happy to be the stay-at-home dog dad.

But then it's a tricky thing: being a feminist and an ally to women willing to do what some would sexistly call *women's work*.

But then also not paying for homeless guys to do my work for me. And also not having a full-time job to actually bring in the money that I then give away to the homeless guys to do my work for me.

Let's make this clear: I do not think my future ex-wife is racist against black guys or home'ist against black homeless guys.

It's more like she's a realist who knows that giving 20 bucks here and there to do yard work or just to get some food is not going to fix the real situation and may actually be making the situation worse by making them think that we will always be here to provide for them.

She calls it enabling.

And *enabling* is a tricky word to argue against when it comes to children, rescue dogs, and homeless people.

We don't have children, but the dogs and the homeless guys are more than enough fodder for marital disagreements.

Which sometimes escalate to loud talking.

Which can sometimes be heard outside our window.

Which I sometimes make the mistake of shushing her.

Which is not a good idea for a man to shush any woman, but especially not his sugar mama.

Me: *But what if they can hear us talking?*

My future ex-wife: *Can… you… hear… me…talking…?*

Which is both fair and unfair and probably a big reason that she's my future ex-wife.

And then there's the dogs. Our dogs.

Barking and barking and barking.

We get mad, they bark.

They bark, my future ex-wife gets mad.

We have a pitbull, a rottweiler/german shepherd mix, and a boykin-chocolate lab mix.

With the pitbull and the rottweiler/german shepherd mix, we have three of the four most popular attack dogs in the world.

And since rottweilers were partially bred with dobermans, we basically have all four of the most popular attack dogs.

And a boykin-chocolate lab that was bred to hunt and bark loud enough to let you know when he's found something dead.

All three of them are rescue dogs so there's that.

But the pride of rescuing dogs from kill shelters gets a little complicated when your dogs look like attack dogs and hunting dogs and do not like black people or homeless people.

Even when the homeless black guys are always acting extra sweet around them and giving them chicken bones to win them over.

Which then makes it complicated for me because I'm left with the decision: do I a). explain that dogs can easily choke on chicken bones? Or b). Thank the homeless black guys for being so nice to my dogs who bark and growl at them when they don't feed them chicken bones.

Oh sorry, you'll have to excuse them. These are all rescue dogs that have been abused and neglected in the past.

That doesn't quite have the same pathos to it when you're explaining it to a bunch of homeless black guys who have to sleep outside a Christ-comma-Scientist church because the homeless shelter doesn't let them drink.

White people and their fuckin dogs.

This is what I imagine Clem, Mel, Mikey, et al. mutter under their breaths when I walk my barking, growling dogs past them twice a day for their twice-a-day walks to keep them from keeping my future ex-wife all night barking.

Or when the dogs are barking at them half the night and my future ex-wife is yelling at me to shut the dogs up or take them outside.

Or when they can hear our TV blaring all night to drown out the sounds of the homeless black guys outside so the dogs don't bark.

And then like every night after midnight listen that Sarah McLachlan commercial come on and it's white people torture porn: *Angel this and angel that and angel angel angel angel, who could ever do something so mean to one of these innocent little sweethearts.*

Waah waah waah, fuckin white people and their fuckin dogs.

It's one of those nights.

Where it's all of the above.

And now the guys outside our window are getting into it. *Motherfucker this.* And *motherfucker that.*

Fuck fuck fuckin cocksucker fuck fuck motherfucker cocksuckin fucker mother shut the fuck up I'll kill you mother fuck.

The barking and the barking and the barking.

My future ex-wife already can't sleep. Even with the central air, it's too hot. It's past midnight and still 80 out at least. The humidity. The dogs and their goddamn hot panting. Me and my goddamn breathing.

She's up reading one of her big WWII books. The ones that she only reads when she's trying to sleep but it's me and the dogs are annoying the shit out of her even though she's the one who has to actually get up in the morning and go to work so I can stay home and feed the dogs and enable the homeless guys and never find a full-time job to pull my own weight.

She's hollering at the dogs to shut the fuck up. She's hollering at me to make the dogs shut the fuck up.

And then the guys outside they're hollering at the dogs to shut the fuck up too.

This is new.

And I can't help but feel a bit betrayed. *After everything I've done for you...* I can't help but think. My white-savior brain feeling a bit butthurt.

Some guys I can't recognize from their voices calling our dogs cocksuckin motherfuckers. And dirty mangy cocksuckin mutts.

It's not really a good situation.

And it's feeling more and more like I am somehow at fault for this situation. Or at least I should be more aware of this.

Like how I should've trained the dogs better—to be less racist and less leery of the homeless and more receptive to commands like *be quiet, BE quiet! shut up, Shut. The. Fuck. Up.* And *Jesus fucking Christ I'm going to murder each and every one of you in your sleep.*

It's not that my future ex-wife wants me to call the cops on them. It's not that she wants me to go threaten them.

This has been the conundrum from the beginning: not pissing off the people who know exactly where you live (and have been allowed inside a few times).

And of course the whole compassion thing for those less fortunate.

My future ex-wife is not a heartless person. She only sometimes comes off as such in the face of an increasingly fraught marriage to a man who has revealed himself to be all pathos, no logos or ethos.

But then there's tonight.

And maybe tonight I can make the right decision and demonstrate some of the qualities that might have attracted her to me in the first place.

Maybe I can save our doomed marriage.

I become decisive. I do not even look out the window. I don't want to let my familiarity with Clem, Mel, Mikey, or anybody else to influence my actions.

This is not okay. And it needs to stop.

I tell myself it's not just my future ex-wife, it's me doing this for the neighborhood. To make them feel safe.

And not just because they are mostly white.

Because I've seen at least a handful of black families in the general area and at least one Hispanic family too. And they are just as likely to be frightened by homeless guys cursing at the top of their lungs. And unlike me who knows these guys are mostly harmless, they are probably considering calling the cops on them.

So I'm doing this for them as much as I am doing this for us and actually I'm doing this for the safety of the homeless guys too because most homeless guys aren't going to be cursing at dogs in the middle of the night. They want peace and quiet to sleep just as much as anybody in a home.

And they might even be more concerned because those shouting guys are even more a threat to them because they are on the front lines.

I decide not to take the dogs outside with me. I don't want to be that white guy with the attack dogs threatening homeless black guys.

I've seen that video go viral too many times.

Fuck you motherfucker, fuck you and fuck you and fuck you. Motherfuckin cocksuckin fuckin fuckin fuck you.

Bark bark bark bark.

I don't take anything else to protect myself either. Not that I own a gun or anything anyway. I don't even own a baseball bat and I'm not about to pull out a big kitchen knife like a psycho.

As soon as the door closes behind me I realize that I haven't put on any clothes. I'm in my boxers and tank top that some people unfortunately still refer to as a *wife-beater*.

But that's okay. Because I do not. Because I am mostly a good-intentioned if highly flawed man.

And because there's no reason for this to come to violence. We're all just humans doing the best we can. We're all just humans with emotions and frustrations that sometimes boil over into real anger when things don't turn our ways.

Hey guys, I say as I round the corner of our place.

It's not Clem, Mel, or Mikey or any of the other guys I know a little, which I should've known it'd never be them in the first place. They wouldn't be cursing at the dogs like that. Acting all crazy and potentially violent.

It's one guy.

One white guy.

One white guy with many opinions.

Looks my age. Though he's clearly had more wear on his treads. A big unkempt beard with wild unkempt hair. A pair of ratty overalls with no undershirt.

I instantly feel sorry for him while simultaneously feeling afraid for myself.

This is Southernass Georgia after all.

The dueling banjos theme from *Deliverance* twangs through my head.

I immediately feel terrible about myself for profiling Southerners.

When he walks out from the shadows of the church awning, I can see his pale freckly arms and armpits under the glare of the streetlight. His reddish-orange nipples.

Hey buddy, I say thinking how: despite the heat around here, I've never seen Clem's or Mel's or Mikey's nipples.

Everything okay? I say thinking: oh okay, at least this won't be about me being a white guy.

He's holding up a bottle in a paper bag. He's taking swigs and pointing it at me and then pointing it at the bedroom where the dogs are barking. Swinging it wildly at the gnats buzzing around his face.

He has snot running down his top lip and lines of spit draped across his beard.

These fucking dogs, man, he says taking a swig and pointing at the dogs and then at me then swinging wildly at the gnats. Fuck you you fucking fuck dogs, he shouts and takes a swig.

Sorry, I say and smile a wry knowing smile. Yeah, they can be pretty annoying sometimes. Just ask my wife, I say and nod back toward the house.

And now I've gone and brought my future ex-wife into things. Who's obviously listening to all this. And thinking oh great, my husband's trying to get me killed too.

They won't shut up about it, the guy says.

About what?

Him.

Who?

Mr. Fishsticks.

Mr. Fishsticks is his cat.

I realize this when he starts looking down the alley and calling, Here Mr. Fishsticks, here kitty, kitty.

We both spend some time looking down the alley and calling for Mr. Fishsticks.

And swatting away gnats.

I say, I'm so sorry about Mr. Fishsticks.

It's not your fault, he says and takes a swig and then wipes his mouth with his pale freckly arm.

It's these fucking dogs.

Bark bark bark fuck you you fuckin cocksuckin fucks.

Hey buddy, I say. I apologize again about Mr. Fishsticks. I ask him if he wants me to help him look some more.

He says, There's no fuckin use. Mr. Fishsticks is never fuckin coming back. Not after these fuckin dogs.

He starts in again on the fuckin cocksuckin dogs.

Nah, nah, I say. He'll come back. He's just scared. He's probably just down the alley away from the dogs.

Then—*ah-hah!*—I hit him with this one: I bet if you found a place away from the dogs, Mr. Fishsticks would find you.

Now I'm a parent trying to trick a child into going to bed.

But that's only because I'm only trying to help reunite him with his beloved Mr. Fishsticks. I'm not simply trying to rid him from my having to confront his clear mental illness and other issues related to his homelessness.

It's a travesty the way our culture deals with mental illness, I tell myself. Just look at this guy. Whatever his name is.

Whatever his name is takes a swig and thinks on it a moment. Swats at the gnats. His eyes watery and bloodshot blinking away the glare of the streetlights.

If it weren't for these goddamn dogs, you know?

I know, I say. These dogs are real assholes.

I'm trying to sound calming and caring without sounding like I'm treating him like a child.

Does he know that these dogs are my dogs? Have I revealed to him that this house is my house, that the wife in question is my future ex-wife?

Your dogs! he spits at me. Your fuckin dogs fuckin scaring my fuckin cat away.

Then: *Here Mr. Fishsticks? Here kitty kitty?*

We go a few more rounds of me apologizing for my dogs and him calling my dogs cocksuckers and me saying how his cat is probably just waiting for him to find a new place to stay away from the scary dogs.

I'm not sure how long it's been. It feels like it's been hours. The gnats are going for my eyes, my mouth, other places down below where I should have pants on.

I can feel the armpit sweat having drenched my sides all the way to my boxers. I can feel my balls sticking to my legs under my boxers.

They are not the boxer briefs that my future ex-wife keeps getting me to get me to stop wearing my old boxers with my penis sticking out when she doesn't want to see it.

At some point the dogs have stopped barking. My future ex-wife may have murdered them (Just kidding, my future ex-wife loves dogs and would never murder them).

But the lights are out. Has she abandoned me? Has she taken the dogs? And abandoned me? Leaving me with nothing but my homeless friends. And this guy. And the gnats.

Hey buddy, I say. I'm so sorry about your cat. But I don't think he's coming back.

I'm trying not to sound terse while also trying to sound more assertive.

Mr. Fishsticks is gone. He's fuckin gone. These fuckin cocksuckin dogs. Your dogs!

He's up in my face now. He's tapping his finger with the bottle into my chest.

His breath does not smell ideal.

I am rethinking my many decisions preceding this. I can hear my future ex-wife in my head listing all the decisions I have made that have led to this situation.

What would she do?

What would she have me do?

He's point-pushing me now with combination fist/finger/brown-bag-liquor-bottle. His bottle of whatever splashing my chest and even my mouth. It tastes like the type of liquor you buy when you are homeless and have no money other than the few dollars some guy like me gives you to ease his conscience.

It's driving the gnats wild.

I have never punched anyone in my life. I've been punched more than a few times. I'm sure I deserved each and every one of them whether it seemed like I deserved them or not.

I'm a lover not a fighter, I used to joke with my future ex-wife when I showed off the various scars I had from being punched.

If you're such a lover of humanity, then why are you getting punched so often?

Touché.

I'm slowly backing up, holding my ground to stop from falling backward but giving ground so to not get knocked over backward.

I have my hands up in the air, the universal signal for *Hey, I don't want to fight you*. I have learned this gesture well over the years. Or not well enough depending on post-punching analysis.

Hey buddy, I keep saying. Easy, man. Everything's cool, dude.

A thought flitters through my brain: Where are the guys when I need them? Clem, Mel, Mikey, and the gang. Every other night, snoring away outside the bedroom window.

I imagine them all of a sudden appearing in the alley and getting in this guy's face.

Hey man, you got a problem with him then you got a problem with us.

The black savior complex to the rescue!

Or else maybe this guy ran them off. Another unhinged racist white dude trying to take his frustrations for his plight in the world out on poor black guys who have it even worse than he does. The way our culture turns poor white people against poor black people.

But here is this dude about to kill me over a cat that very likely is just a delusion and Clem, Mel, and Mikey are nowhere to be seen.

Hey man! I say and hold my ground finally.

I'm not your enemy.

You want me to help you find your cat, I'll stay here all night and help you find your cat.

I don't want to fight you.

But just don't make me have to call the cops on you.

You keep coming at me like this, I'm sorry, but I'm gonna have to call the cops.

For your safety as well as mine.

Dude is crying now. He's leaning up against my house and crying and collapsing down to the ground.

Mr. Fishsticks, he cries and takes a sad swig of hopefully the end of it.

Mr. Fishsticks.

You know where he is?

He's not fuckin nowhere, that's where.

He's fuckin gone.

He's fuckin dead.

I killed him and now he's dead and he's never fuckin comin back.

I'm sorry, I say.

I have real trepidations about it but I do it anyway. I lean over and put my hand on his shoulders.

That sucks man, I say. But it's not your fault.

I fuckin killed him, man. I fuckin killed him so bad he'll never come back to me.

I say I'm sorry again. And it's not your fault. I say how he probably didn't mean it and how things just happen sometimes. Bad things to good people. It's just the world we live in and the world's not fair sometimes.

What I'm thinking as I'm saying this is: How many gnats have I swallowed? How chafed am I between my thighs? I'm thinking it's been a long night and I'm tired and my future ex-wife has probably been asleep since the moment the dogs stopped barking. She's not hearing any of this. All the things I'm saying to this guy who clearly needs help, but how much is my help going to really help in the long run.

Will he even remember this tomorrow morning? Will he even remember this an hour from now?

When people ask him about his lost cat, will he remember to mention how consoling that random stranger was? How kind and patient and understanding.

And where are the guys anyway? What did he do to them to run them off?

It's a tricky situation. Do I keep helping this guy who probably doesn't even have a cat and very likely might have threatened to kill all the black homeless guys, some of them kind of being like friends to me?

Or do I just call the cops?

For his benefit and for mine.

Get him a place to sleep and something to eat. Hopefully, get him some treatment even though that probably won't happen, the way cops deal with guys like this with real mental health issues.

But that doesn't mean they won't get him help.

Believe in the good in people and you will find the good in them.

Whoever said that.

Hey buddy, I say. I touch his bare shoulder. I squeeze comfortingly. Feel his sweat and warmth and fatigue in it.

Hey, buddy, I say. I squeeze his shoulder a little more forcefully.

Uh-mm, he says. Mm-uh, he says.

Then he falls over on his side.

And spills the rest of his liquor all down his cover-all crotch.

And vomits.

And starts snoring.

I think about waking him up to get him back over under the awning. I think about the various reactions that might get from him.

He's snoring but in a kind of cute way. Like a big baby. A big sweaty stinky baby with violent tendencies drenched with liquor and regurgitated liquor.

What was I supposed to do? I imagine myself telling my future ex-wife the next morning.

You should've seen him sleeping there. He was harmless. He'd just lost his cat.

Leaving out the part where he may have murdered Mr. Fishsticks.

Me making the case: Can't you even imagine losing the only good thing you had in this world? Imagine one of our dogs running away and think about all we have and he doesn't. And we have two more dogs. And each other.

To be clear: my future ex-wife is not a cold and uncompassionate woman. She is just a woman with a lot on her plate. A woman who can't sleep most nights with how hot it is and three barking dogs. And a husband who doesn't always make it easy.

A woman who has to turn to Hitler to put her mind to rest. How sad is that?

And me.

My only friends, a handful of homeless guys who probably only talk to me because I pay them to.

The dogs I feed and walk and let them sleep in the bed with me, dogs that we rescued from kill shelters, and all that and how happy are they, really? The way they act like they'd rip a man from limb to limb just for being black and/or homeless.

It's so true.

Hurt people hurt people.

And dogs.

Is it the right thing to do—to call the cops to come get this guy? For whom is it the right thing to do? For me? My not-yet ex-wife? For Clem, et al?

For this guy who needs help but is probably not going to get it?

You know who he's not going to get any help from? Jesus fucking Christ—*comma*—the Scientist. And not from any of his hypocritical self-righteous followers either.

And while we're at it, not from Tom Cruise, John Travolta, or any of those Scientology psychos.

But who am I really to judge? Who am I to tell them what to believe or who to believe in?

It's just a tough situation all around.

That's what I tell myself. Over and over. Until my wife wakes up the next morning and I make her favorite breakfast: omelet, extra cheese, with scallions on top.

So you called the cops?

Yeah, I know. I didn't know what else to do. It was just a tough situation all the way around, you know?

She has things to say about that and I wait and listen patiently and apologize for everything I've put her through until she eventually leaves for work.

I take the dogs out for their morning walk.

Nobody at the Christ-comma-Scientist church to talk to or scare away.

NURSE BERNIE

NURSE BERNIE SAYS my not wanting to ever have children—never ever ever—is selfish, nothing more to it.

She calls me honey.

Honey, she says and pats my thigh, good god-fearin people need to populate the world with good god-fearin babies.

All these white people with too much time on their hands. Overthinkin everything, that's what's wrong with people these days.

Nurse Bernie's my therapist or at least the registered nurse I go to to get my prescriptions filled for my happy pills because Dr. Samuels my actual therapist never has time to see me.

Nurse Bernie's way better anyway.

She's black and has lots of things to say about uppity liberal white people.

I'm not sure if this includes me or not—in real life and/or in her mind.

And either way, I'm here for it.

Anytime I can listen to an older black lady tell me what's wrong with me and all my uppity white brethren, I'm all ears.

Nurse Bernie says all these white people around here with their uppity opinions can pull her gun from her cold dead hand.

She says her daddy taught her to shoot a pistol when she was eight and she's been packing ever since he got shot in an argument over who's turn it was to pay alimony—him or her mama, who he'd also taught to shoot.

If she remembers that I'm here for treatment because of my PTSD from my brother shooting himself, she doesn't mention it.

She says all the white people around here are trying to drive her crazy.

But it's not just white people.

Her kids are trying to drive her crazy.

That girl's gonna mess around and wind up with a 501 involuntary intake in her honor and I'm not gonna sign her out.

The boy, now he's a lost cause.

Too much of his dad in him.

That deadbeat son of a bitch.

My therapist is not actually a therapist, is a registered nurse who gets to dole out pills and opinions but has to get it signed off on by an old white psychiatrist named Doctor Purvis.

Not that being a registered nurse isn't just as honorable as being a psychiatrist.

I've seen a lot of psychiatrists—most of them uppity old white men like Doctor Purvis.

Most of these uppity old white male psychiatrists haven't been all that honorable or empathetic as far as I'm concerned.

But I'm not sure what to call Bernie if I can't call her Dr.

Bernie? Nurse Bernie? Miss Bernie?

I want to show respect, but I don't want to be patronizing.

The staff at the clinic all calls her Miss Bernie, but they're all southern black ladies.

And I'm not southern. Or black. Or a lady.

Bernie says the lady with the kid who comes in before me, she refuses to tell the little brat no.

Someday he'll be in the paper for burning down the house and that mother'll be in the background saying that's okay, that's okay, it wasn't your fault.

Parents these days.

Bernie has a little framed poster that says, *If I wasn't running late all the time, I'd never get any exercise.*

When she runs late, I get to sit for hours in the waiting room with the kids and their parents and the non-kid, non-parent patients.

We watch *Full House,* but not reruns.

The new ones.

The ones without the Olson twins.

We do not watch them on mute. We watch them on full volume.

The kids playing their video games with the sound turned up.

The parents of the kids telling their kids to turn the damn volume down.

In between their texting and scrolling social media.

And their parents' texting and scrolling on social media.

The non-kid, non-parents rocking in their chairs, mumbling, rubbing their fingertips for nicotine.

I'm feeling guilty just for being here.

I'm a privileged cis-hetero white dude with privileged cis-hetero-white-dude problems.

Things like anxiety and depression and separation anxiety.

Survivor's guilt.

Post-traumatic stress disorder.

I'm not a vet. I haven't been to war. Nobody's ever tried to murder me in a dark alley.

There's the thing with my brother shooting himself in the room next to mine. And the thing with me accidentally burning my family's house down while masturbating when I was fourteen.

That's all.

But apparently these days anything counts from PTSD.

Suicide: the ultimate privileged-cis-hetero-white-dude problem.

Waah waah, nobody knows how hard we have it.

Get on in here already, Big Ben, Bernie says with a big smile.

She's a half-hour behind.

Because she was a half-hour late.

By the end of the day she'll be an hour behind.

I once sat and watched *Fuller House* with the mental defect crowd for two hours waiting to get my prescriptions renewed.

Lord Jesus, these people are gonna drive me crazy, Nurse Bernie says.

She tells me about what the kid before me has done now and what the mom hasn't done.

She says if it weren't for Trazodone she'd never get a night's sleep.

Trazodone take me away, she says, leaning back in her chair as if she's taking a bath.

I say sorry. That sounds like a tough way to make it through.

I'm constantly telling her sorry.

And qualifying how stupid and petty all my problems are.

How privileged I am and how guilty I feel even having to come here.

She says, Oh honey.

She says, Bless your heart.

She says, Baby, if all my patients were as easy as you…

She says, In therapy there's no such thing as white people problems and black people problems. There's just problems and finding ways to cope with those problems.

And now I've gone and done it again: made an educated black woman tell me that my problems are just as valid as black people's problems.

It's like saying an offensive joke to your black friend and then apologizing so profusely that they have to make you feel better about saying they were just being overly sensitive to your racist joke.

She asks if we haven't tried [these pills] yet? [Those pills]? How about [them other pills]?
We have.
Really? she says. I could'a sworn.
I'm running out of pills to try but she'll never admit defeat.
Well, she says, I guess we're back to step 1. Step 1 times 2.
She tells me, Don't you go giving up on me yet.
She says, You think you can get rid of me that easy, baby? Just ask my ungrateful kids.
This is comforting to me.
I have a real fear of abandonment and Bernie does a good job of comforting me like that.
Until she doesn't.
Until Bernie finally goes and gives up on me.
For good.
The day I show up and wait and wait and wait and Bernie doesn't show up late.
She doesn't show up at all.
I sign my name to the sign-in sheet and the black lady behind the desk looks at it and then looks at me and gives me the hmmmm face.
It's not that I don't know her name.
Her name is Regina.
Regina with the hmmmm face says, Oh baby, oh honey, didn't you hear?
I shrug.
Regina says, Miss Bernie, she's no longer with us.
I look at her.
I mean, she's moved on.
I look at her.
No, she says, picking up on my look. She's not dead, baby. She just gave her notice on Friday.
I say: And nobody called me?
Regina says, It was a surprise to all of us.

I say, Oh, sorry.

I look at Regina.

Regina looks at me with her hmmmm face.

We don't say it, but we both understand it implicitly.

These damn people have finally done drove Miss Bernie crazy.

Regina says Dr. Samuels is covering for Miss Bernie for the time being.

Do you want to see Dr. Samuels?

No, no I don't want to see Dr. Samuels.

I just want my Nurse Bernie and I want to tell her I'm not done with her. I still need her. You can't get rid of me this easily.

Just ask my ex-wife.

Wouldn't Nurse Bernie laugh at that? Laugh and feel not so bad about abandoning me.

Of course I end up with Dr. Samuels. Because there's only one Nurse Bernie. And because white-man PTSD is real as much as any other white-man neuroses. Same as survivor's guilt. Same as fear of abandonment.

And because I need my happy pills.

And because Nurse Bernie in her rush to leave, didn't leave me any forwarding address for search and rescue.

I wonder and wonder to this day, Did it actually happen? Did I finally wear her out? Did she finally get sick and tired of trying to make me feel better about my white-man problems?

Or did her damn ungrateful kids go and kill her? And did they pull her gun out of her cold dead hands when they did it?

Or did she just have a nervous breakdown and threaten to shoot her boss?

Oh the wonders with Nurse Bernie, oh they will never cease to amaze me.

ROADRAGE LADY

ON MY WAY BACK from dropping my wife off at the airport last night a lady tailgates me for 45 minutes.

I speed up. I slow down. I pull off into a gas station.

She stays five feet off my bumper all the way back to town.

My fragile masculinity wants me to point out that it's dark out, that I don't know it's a lady.

That had I known it was *just a lady* I would've pulled over and told her to get off my dick.

But this is Southernass Georgia where everybody carries a gun. Except me.

Everybody including a middle-aged black lady driving a lipstick-red Ford Fusion.

So there's that.

And the potential of drugs.

And old garden-variety craziness.

Not that you have to be a *crazy lady* in order to follow a man 45 minutes out of your way.

Maybe I had cut her off?

Maybe I had accidentally run her off the road?

Maybe someone driving a similarly beige Honda CRV had kidnapped her child never to be seen again?

And, honestly, who am I to be trusted with this story or any other story?

She follows me from the exit onto the interstate.

She follows me from the exit off the interstate.

Follows me another 20 miles into town.

To the hospital a mile away from my place.

Follows me all the way to the cop I flag down at the hospital.

Idles there six inches off my back bumper while I explain to the cop that this lipstick-red Ford Fusion has been on my ass for 45 minutes.

I don't know it's just one lady yet.

I don't know if that lady yet knows that I am a five-eleven, 300-pound man with what I think is a pretty intimidating fu manchu and mohawk.

Or if she'll care one way or another.

But the cop knows.

Sorry, officer, this might sound stupid, but I'm worried they might have a gun.

This is my fragile masculinity doing the talking.

This is the cop, the 20-, maybe 30-year-old black female cop looking me up and down.

This is the black female cop looking back at the middle-aged black lady in the Ford Fusion idling six inches off my ass.

This is the black female cop acknowledging my fragile white male ego: Mm-hmm. Okay. Let me see.

This is the black female cop returning from her talk with the middle-aged black lady behind me: The lady says you were following her. She says she only followed you to teach you a lesson.

Is she crazy?

Is she on drugs?

Does she have a gun?

I don't ask those questions.

Nor does my fragile white male ego.

It seems like an innocent misunderstanding.

This is what she doesn't say: *Sir, it seems like you're a big fat racist pussy.*

She says, Do you feel comfortable driving home on your own? Or would you like an officer to accompany you?

What if she has taken down my license plate so she can track me down and murder me and my dogs with a machete in the middle of the night?

What if she is the main squeeze of the head of a neo-nazi outlaw biker gang that goes by the moniker The Southern Crosses?

No, I say. As long as she doesn't follow me.

Mm-hmm, the black female cop says. I think you'll be fine.

But I am not fine.

I do not have a gun.

I am not dead (as of this writing).

But I am far far far away from fine.

But I want you to know it has nothing to do with my bruised white male ego.

I want you to know that I am a feminist.

I'd like you to believe I'm an anti-racist.

A Blacktivist.

Despite me being the whitest man ever.

That I believe middle-aged black ladies can be the head of their own neo-nazi outlaw biker gangs.

Just as 25-year-old black women can be fine policewomen—no, check that, police *officers*—who can serve and protect as good or better than any man, and keep you safe, no matter what they might think of your fragile male ego.

Just as a black woman doesn't need to be *crazy* to follow you home.

I'd like you to know that though I support all Tyler Perry has done to promote black culture on TV and in movies, I find his portrayal of the archetypal hysterically angry black woman problematic.

Crazy is a prejudice.

Crazy can be a simple misunderstanding.

Or it can be that you have kidnapped and murdered a woman's child and have completely repressed it only to have it creep up in your thoughts on long dark stretches of the highway with too much time to think about everything you've done wrong in your life, every failure, and what fate you might deserve.

Just so long as the women in your life do not take it out on your dogs.

Your friends, best friends, only friends, all of them male, all of them big and scary-looking dogs but deep down complete teddy bears who'd never hurt a fly and are not threatened by dominant women of any race.

Your dog best friends having learned this from your all-powerful wife, soon-to-be-ex-wife.

HONEY BABY DARLIN SWEETIE PIE

I HAVEN'T BEEN DOWN HERE LONG, but I immediately recognize the look on this peckerwood's face.

This 12-year-old car salesperson, his mommy the manager and daddy dearest the owner and operator.

This chip-off-the-old-block peckerwood having just informed this elderly black lady that they'll get to her car when they get to her car. But not til the end of the day

The way that that old black lady side-eyes that peckerwood, this is what I'm here for. This is how a boring day at the mechanic's suddenly becomes popcorn theater.

Old lady waits a moment side-eyeing him even harder. Waiting for him to say, Oh, sorry, I didn't know it was you, Miss [Insert Name Who Happens to Be Related to My Mother's Aunt's Best Friend's Choir Director]. No, no, no for you Ma'am, we'll have it ready in a jiff.

She waits in vain.

Uh-uh, she says, ain't nobody leavin me here stranded. Then side-eyeing over to her sleepy husband not paying attention: Lester, you get the car.

This peckerwood car sales kid might give her an eye roll but then it's all yes-ma'am, no ma'am, sorry ma'am, I'll do the best I can, ma'am.

Up North, it was Ben. Or Drevlow. Or Mr. D if they were trying to be formal.

Down here I'm nothing but yes-sir, no-sir.

Mister Ben to all my students.

Any woman over 30 and it's honey, baby, darlin, sweetie pie.

Oh baby, bless your heart, the secretary at school always tells me when I ask a stupid question.

My favorite, the black lady at McDonalds, my same age, always calling me baby when she hands me my 20-piece nugget, double-quarter-pounder supersize-me fries and Oreo McFlurry.

It's amazing how far baby, honey, darlin, sweetie pie will get you down here.

How nobody will ever apologize for taking 20 minutes to four hours longer than expected or required, but they all know my name and tell me to have a blessed day and/or y'all come back now, y'hear.

That's how much they love me, how much there is to love me, I'm literally *y'all*.

There's the way locals chew vowels and spit them out of the side of their mouths like snuff. *Bean*, they call me. It's not a nickname. It's how they say my name. And I love it.

They can add anywhere from two to four more syllables to my last name than necessary: Dreevellow? Drevloo-oh? Dirrevelloon?

Until I got down here I was convinced there was only one way to pronounce *Drevlow* and it was *Drev-low*.

The other day a large woman stopped in the middle of the turning lane on Main Street and shook her head at me.

Sheeeee't, she says. Honey, you always walkin them dang dogs and they always walkin you. Bless your heart, she says.

I laugh a little politely, say thanks. Give her the two-finger wave. On with our days. A little happier than before.

They got this football coach down here. Won like eight championships for the college team in the 80s.

His name was Eric Russell.

Except you ask about Eric Russell and everybody'll say, Who you talkin about now?

Because everybody calls him *Irk*.

The way it oughta be.

The college I teach at has signs all over the place that say *GATA*. It took me two and a half years to realize it was an acronym for *Get After Their Asses* or more colloquially *Git After They Asses* (though the school officially says *Get After Them Aggressively* or even worse: *Get After Those Academics*).

This all being part of Irk's big pre-game peptalk.

Get after they asses, boys!

They might not like the gays down here but they're nothing if not proud to *git after they ass good and hard*.

Up North, my people have their opinions too. But they speak their racism and homophobia straight up their nose. I'm half-Norwegian and half-German and I talk straight through my nose. My wife used to make fun of me for saying bags *bAAAgs* and eggs *AAAggs*.

Up North they're always bitchin about all these new hifalutin reality shows starring *the gays*.

I've started saying *y'all* instead of *you guys* or *you's guys* to be more inclusive. It feels good, like a big old loogie oozing down the back of my tongue and on out the corner of my mouth.

Who would've thought that Southerners had figured out a gender-neutral pronoun all this time while Northerners were bending over backwards to call themselves woke?

Places like where I'm from in Northernass Wisconsin where everybody wants to claim their wokeness in comparison.

When mostly everybody's racist in theory up there.

As in: *We don't actually have any black people up North but we're still a little worried about that gangsta rap we've heard about on the teevee.*

I probably don't have to mention names like George Floyd, Armando Castillo, and Jacob Black.

But I will.

If you haven't seen the news, then let me just inform you that if you come to the North you can shoot a BLM protestor and be hailed a hero.

That's how woke it is up where I'm from.

I've always talked slow and a little bit slurry and mumbly. My ex-wife was always yelling at me to articulate.

My high school English teacher once had me get checked for a speech impediment, though a speech impediment is nothing to feel bad about, it's a thing that's gonna get you made fun of, especially up North when everybody talks in short, clipped syllables so as to not freeze to death when rambling on about how shitty the weather is.

I've spent my whole life looking for people who understand me.

I haven't found them yet, but what I've realized now is all I really need is for people to pretend and nod along and call me honey and baby and never ask me to repeat myself and love me forever no matter what dumb shit might come out my mouth.

This peckerwood car salesman comes up to me and tells me it's gonna be another couple hours for them to check my oil.

He calls it *ohlllll*.

I've already been here two hours.

Doesn't even hit me with the yes sir, no sir, so sorry sir.

I make eyes around the place looking for somebody else to acknowledge this youngin's lack of Southern manners.

Everybody else's nose in a paper or magazine or watching Fox News on silent TV.

Uh-uh, I say and side-eye that old black lady who doesn't side-eye me back. Bless your heart, boy. Ain't nobody leavin me sittin here for two hours for some little old ohlll change.

The peckerwood just shrugs at me and goes back to get his manager.

Comes back with some middle-aged white lady who could be his mother if it weren't for the lack of manners he's shown, lack of respect for his elders.

They have this expression down here: *get above your raisin*.

For a long time I thought it had something to do with raisins, but it turned out no.

Well, I've been here long enough now to know this peckerwood has clearly gotten above his raisin.

His mother: Honey, can't you see all these good kind people waiting patiently with you?

Bless your heart, baby, your car's gon get done when it's done. Same as all these other kind beautiful folks.

But in the meantime, can I offer you some sweet tea and fresh donuts, hon?

The way you're talkin to my Johnny here, you look like you might could use some nourishment to put you in a better mood.

Honey, she says, holding up the donuts and sweet tea, you can't help but put a smile on your face you get some some good old fashioned sweat tea and donuts in you.

And she's right. Bless her heart, I really could go for some sweet tea and donuts.

HAROLD & REGGIE

SOMEBODY'S GONE AND GOTTEN STUCK in our front yard again.

We've moved way the fuck away from the Christ, Science church but now we live on one of those random four-way stops in the middle of a random neighborhood that everybody runs because they think nobody else is coming.

It's this old guy. Crashes his taxi over the curb. He doesn't wreck or anything.

It's rained earlier so everything's soft and messy.

Other than two big ruts, it mostly just makes the yard look more lived-in than it already looks.

The neighbor kittycorner to the right parks her school bus on her front lawn and wakes me up every morning with the backing alarm.

The neighbor across the street drives a tow truck and wakes me up every night to the backing alarm.

Nobody's calling any HOA's.

My dogs are barking.

I'm out there being a good samaritan at two in the morning and the guy keeps on calling me big boy.

Because I'm not skinny and I'm in my forties.

And he's skinny and in his sixties.

Hey big boy, he says kicking his front tire.

How's about giving an old man a hand here. Son of a bitch snuck right up on me.

My dogs won't stop barking (not a euphemism).

Other dogs from around the neighborhood join in on the barking.

I had just gone back to sleep from the tow truck guy backing in.

I'm in my threadbare, pit-stained wifebeater and those night pants my ex-wife got me so I'd stop walking around the house free-balling.

They're red patterned with white dog bones all over them.

I never did figure out the meaning behind them, but I'm buttass naked less and less these days.

I don't have anything underneath so if one was to look with the flashers in just the right spot, one could see some of my dog bones that not even my ex-wife wanted to see.

I look over at the towtruck guy's house.

No lights.

I look over at the school bus lady's house.

No lights.

I look at the old guy, on the phone now hollering lies at somebody for why he isn't picking somebody else up.

The front tire shredded.

Son of a bitch just snuck right up on me, the old guy says.

I'm white and he's black and I feel a little awkward being the young white guy to fix the old black guy's tire and worrying that somebody from where I teach might think I'm white-savioring him, instead of just being neighborly.

I'm not some crazy conservative alt righty, but this is the Southernass Georgia, and I'm from the Northernass Wisconsin and have a masters in English. I'm not about to tell anybody this story and include the fact that I'm technically speaking a *Master in English*.

Plus there's the fact that the old man's been drinking.

I'm still learning things about what's appropriate via race relations versus what's southern hospitality.

Yessir, nosir, Be happy to, sir.

I don't at all smell the alcohol on your breath or blame it for your plight tonight and I will never include this detail when I relay this story, in fact I won't even mention that you were black because what does color matter in a time of need.

Mostly I'm just not wanting to have any police come and then the tow truck guy come and people asking everybody questions about what they been drinking or smoking and driving all over the lawn.

There's lived-in and then there's trying to mow the lawn all lumpy and bumpy and sending grass and sand from anthills flying this way and that.

The wheel's in deep, the undercarriage, maybe two inches off the grass.

Soft sand, I have to shovel about a foot of lawn out just to get the jack in.

The dogs are gonna have a field day re-digging this hole for a cooling pit.

If the fire ants don't get to it first.

His jack looks like it's from the 1920s.

I use my jack.

How's she coming, big boy? he says in between calling lies to other people.

My jack's about buried, I've shoveled down as deep as I can shovel for the jack to touch.

You need a plank or something, big boy. You ain't got a plank?

If I was older and wiser I would've thought to get a plank to prop up the jack.

I shrug. It's dark out. He's not paying attention anyway.

It's too late for a plank.

I'm in too deep for a plank.

No, where we are right now, we're at an impasse.

The dogs barking barking barking, pawing the shit out of the front door.

Those your dogs?

I used to have a dog.

Blind dog.

Furry little fucker'd keep me up all day all night barking at the dark.

Put that damn dog down the first time he shit the bed.

Nuh-uh. Never again, I told my wife. No goddamn barking dogs.

I say sorry, they're just stressed out after the storm.

Ain't no need to be sorry, big boy.

They ain't my dogs. I ain't your neighbor.

Fix that tire and we'll call it a happy night.

It takes a while.

I get my white tank top with the unfortunate colloquial name soaked with sweat, my hands all greasy, my dog-bone pants all grass-stained, sand grinding around up in my kibbles and bits.

A few people drive by, ask if they can help.

Ah that's mighty kind of you, sir, but don't you worry, me and the boy, we got it covered.

None of them are a tow truck.

None of them are somebody from the taxi company coming to help.

I'm half expecting the sun to come up by the time I wrangle the wheel off, wrangle the spare on.

Dawn before I get the lug nuts tightened.

The old man telling somebody that somebody's gonna have to cover somebody's picking up somebody else's fair.

Why look at you, big boy, he says putting his hand over the receiver. Shit if I wasn't sure I was gonna have to call some degenerate redneck to charge me an arm and a leg to tell me what I done wrong.

But here you come to save the day.

Gives me a tender kick to the ass of my dog bone pants.

It is quite an accomplishment, really.

Plank or no plank, I'm feeling pretty good about my problem solving.

And for being neighborly.

And color blind.

If only my Midwestern friends could see how two southern gentlemen can put race and age aside and be neighborly when it counts.

Then some guy in another taxi pulls up.

Different company.

That you, Harold?

Who's that?

Reggie.

Reggie who?

Reggie Watkins.

Shit, Reggie Watkins, I thought you was the cops all creeping up on me.

You remember, me. We went to second grade together.

I member old Miss Mavis and me putting gum on her seat that day. I member little punk by name of Reggie Watkins snitching on me.

You been drinking, Harold?

Shit, I know you been drinking.

Shit, I'm just trying to help a brother out.

You best get your ass home, Reg, you know what's good for you.

You know what's good for you, you'd've called a guy like me to help your ass in the first place. Get you out before the police come asking their questions and barking their orders.

Shit, I'd've called you and you'd've been the one snitching on me, Reg, you snitchinass punk motherfucker.

I'm putting the flat in the back of the taxi.

I'm waiting for Harold to tell Reggie that he sure lucked out and that big white boy really saved his ass and it turns out they're not all racist republicans after all.

He doesn't.

You good though?

Shit, I'm good, Reg. You good?

You need me to call somebody?

Nah, man, I got this shit covered. Nothing but the Lord challenging me to find the straight and narrow.

Amen to that.

Amen to that.

All right then.

All right then

I'm unscrewing my jack when Reggie honks and drives off.

The dogs go back to barking, scratching the pain off the door.

I kick the tire, start to say, Think you're good to go, sir.

He says, Hold on there, big boy.

Don't you go abandoning me now.

Leave me here spinning in quicksand the rest of the night.

He means for me to push him out.

The sky is almost blue, my back is hurting, and my ego is deflating by the minute.

I'm making a thing of holding my back and slouching off to one side.

He's walking around inspecting the car as if I'm the one to wreck it.

Over his shoulder I see the bus driver lady coming out to start up the bus.

She's giving us major stink eye.

I'd like to think it's the dog's barking pissing her off, or just the what-the-fuck happened now hairy eyeball, but I'm not unconvinced that she's a bit racist.

I wave and smile and get my second wind.

White guilt can be a powerful motivating factor in proving you're not racist like your neighbors.

Harold's in the car, revving it, but not spinning the tires.

You're almost done, big boy. Get you a big old breakfast to reward yourself.

He's not offering to buy. Just floating the idea that I've earned my calories and fat content this morning.

And I have.

Back cockeyed, I limp around to the rear bumper, wince and get low.

There's spinning and sand flying in my face.

I'm trying to rock it and he's trying to gun it.

I keep hollering to ease up and then go.

He keeps hollering back.

You ain't got no kitty litter?

You ain't got no extra gravel?

You don't got a hitch on that car of yours?

I don't.

Well, you best put your back into it then, big boy.

I'll give her all she's got.

Neighbors are starting to come out and get their paper, let their dogs out.

Starting to gawk.

Y'all want me out of your neighborhood, he hollers, feel free to come over and start pushing.

Harold doesn't get out of the car to help push on the front door the way most people do.

He sits there giving her and giving it to me and giving it to everybody watching.

But lady beep-beep-beeps and then pulls away, never offering to give tow.

I'm almost down in the fetal position rocking rocking with my ailing back up against the bumper as low as I can go.

My dogs are barking big time. And I mean that in all the ways.

I ain't in shape for this kind of shit. I ain't in shape for pretty much any kind of shit.

But still I rock trying to win one for civil rights and post-racial America.

A one and a two and a three…
A one and a two and a three…
You motherfuckin…
Cocksuckin…
Son of a bitchin…
And then by some fluke she finally catches.

Ka-thunk-a-thunk over the ruts and the sidewalk, scraping the undercarriage and then squealing the tires on the pavement.

I collapse on my back and just lie there a minute imagining who might come and take me to the hospital if I can't get up.

Not Harold.

Not that he's forgotten me.

It's a honk and wave for Harold.

Bless your heart, big boy, he hollers.

Or rather he hollers something I can't hear from over the honking.

I'm left to choose his niceties for him, I'm left to fill in the blessings and the amens.

The way I choose to think it'd been a stray dog he'd swerved to miss only to end up in my lawn.

And not just the drinking.

Or the telling lies on his phone.

Maybe a stray dog that could not get rescued and bark their heads off potential threats to their owner's safety the way my mutts were barking after my safety, the way dogs don't always do well when it comes to race relations.

This is water. This is water.

This speech I sometimes give my students about giving people the benefit of the doubt. Of imagining that this might be their worst day and sometimes we forget the obvious thins in this world and need reminding.

Good people have bad days. Good people lose their tempers. Good people sometimes forget to properly reward the hustle.

And sometimes good people have good goddamn reasons to hightail it out of a tough spot in a whiteass neighborhood where some racist lady is just waiting to call the cops on you for drinking and wrecking.

This is water, the way I choose to think he'll be telling whoever he goes home to what a nice young man it was to come out in the middle of the night and get him out of the shit so he doesn't get fired from being a taxi-driver.

The way I choose to think that I'm just a good southern gentleman who respects his elders.

And not another fragile-ego'ed white savior looking for someone to celebrate my achievements in race relations.

I'm thinking this right up to the moment I'm about to drift off to sleep in the bathtub, vanilla bath salts soothing by bad back, by aching knees.

Right up to the moment school bus lady comes back from her morning runs.

Beep-beep-beep.

The dogs barking once again.

Somewhere a stranded somebody waiting for a taxi ride that'll never come.

Somebody on the phone yelling at somebody else.

What'ch you think? I was trying to wreck just to rehab my bad back?

Son of a bitch just snuck up on me.

No, I ain't been drinking.

It wasn't for some big white boy with his shovel and jack, who knows how long I might've been stuck in the mud.

No help from you.

No help from Reggie.

You know Reggie.

Reggie from second grade.

Hell, how should I remember if he was the one with the good-looking sister.

Shit, you ain't pay me enough for this.

You want you go get that fair yourself.

I'm too old for all this haggling and finagling.

Some people, they ain't got no respect for their elders.

Some people, they think every n-word's out there trying to break their backs for 50 acres and mule.

Well, shit, I ain't no n-word and they sure as hell ain't my master.

And me? I'm thinking this is water, this is water, while I soak in my bath salts and think out this whole time I'm thinking all this, you tell them, Harold. Fuck white people, Harold. Fuck these wannabe masters.

But then I get to thinking, fuck me, a guy just trying to give a guy the benefit of a doubt and even then my *this is water* ends up tainted by race and stereotypes.

And I think, shit, this whole story it's not about race at all. Not about me saving some guy from getting the cops called on him. Not about some old guy driving taxi on the night shift just to make a buck, long after he should've been tired.

This whole story's about dogs.

Dogs and people and the shit we do to each other and all because we're insecure and afraid and sometimes that all turns into a bunch of territorial bullshit.

Except even that doesn't hold up.

Dogs, they get to sniff each other's junk, see who they really are underneath all the hackles and tail-wagging, and get on with humping and wrestling and running shit around the sandy, rutty tore up yard.

Wherever you are, Harold, I'm sorry.

I'm sorry for this story and I'm sorry for every story every racistass whiteass motherfuckin honky has ever told about you getting caught in wrong neighborhood.

BENJAMIN/BENJAMIN

DUDE KEEPS SAYING HEY BUDDY, hey buddy buddy, until I turn around.

He points at his name tag: *Hello my name is JORDAN BENJAMIN.*

Then points at mine. *Hello my name is BENJAMIN DREVLOW.*

Crazy, right, bro?

This is our meet-cute.

He rolls his tongue inside his lower lip:

I seen you everywhere, big boy.

All of you.

Your asscrack on up to your cookie pouch.

He pauses and eyes me up and down as if he's seen more but is gonna keep that to himself.

For the time being.

He licks the pencil mustache on his upper lip.

Don't take it personal, he says.

I take it personal.

I feel like he might be coming on to me.

In my book that's personal.

I'm not gay but I'm game if people are into me.

By *game* I mean *dtf*.

Down to flirt.

I'm full of mixed messages is what I mean.

He segues into his memoirs.

He calls them mem-wahs.

I've seen some dark shit, he says.

He says it again whispering up close: *Dark. Shit.*

He's a veteran.

A wounded soldier.

Some ribbons, some awards.

I don't remember.

He almost died in a car accident.

The car accident having nothing to do with his being a veteran.

He tells me, I write so I don't dream, you dig?

You know anything about that, big boy?

It's kind of a narrative jump from how we got to his car crash from his time in the military.

He shows me photos even though I'm more than happy to take him at his word.

He wasn't supposed to survive.

Wasn't supposed to walk again.

He had brain damage.

He was partially paralyzed.

He gives me a pelvic thrust. Slaps his thighs.

Taught himself to walk again. He slaps his head. He taught himself to talk again, to think again, yadda yadda.

He licks his lips and wrinkles up his little mustache. Does the subtlest of pelvic thrusts when he says he's seen all of me everywhere.

He is short and curvaceous and black and has long straightened hair.

I am large and white and have a mowhawk.

I'm like Whitman, I tell him. *Mere clothes cannot contain my multitudes.*

I lean in. I wink.

I can't help how much love I exude. I'm always in danger of exploding.

I don't say any of that.

I say I'm sorry and tug at the bottom of my shirt.

Don't apologize, he says.

I told you don't take it personal.

His breath smells like spearmint. He isn't chewing gum. I see no mints in there.

I'm not going to tell you the flavor of cologne he's wearing.

But just imagine for a moment he isn't wearing cologne.
Imagine I'm not wearing deodorant.
Imagine it's nothing but our man musk, our animal magnetism.
Imagine he isn't black and I'm not white and we aren't talking at a writing conference. We're making sweet tender love in a hot tub full of turkey gravy.
And now all this is a true story and we're consuming each other's trauma.
And we're crying and giggling with each delicious mouthful.
Imagine we're anything other than: one forward black man and one shy awkward fat white dude.
Too shy to take things in anyway other than personal.
Too insecure not to pull my shirt down and pants up as I turn my back on love as quick as I can.
Anyway, I thought you should know, he tells me and turns away and is never to be seen or heard from again.
Or maybe not.
Again can be a lifetime
Again can be tomorrow.
It all depends.
Some of us get what we deserve in this life.
Some of us get what we deserve in this life.

[NAME REDACTED]

I ASK [NAME REDACTED] why he isn't working with his group.

[Name Redacted] says he's reading about Jesus.

It doesn't look like any bible I've ever seen.

It looks more like an alt weekly zine.

I tell [Name Redacted] it's group work time now, not reading time.

He says, What's the problem, man? I can't read about fuckin Jesus? I'm just reading about fuckin Jesus, here. Is that some big problem with you, bro?

He's six-three, black, 18 years old.

I'm five eleven, white, 45 years old.

I say, No no, that's fine, Jesus is fine, but maybe let's talk about it outside.

[Name Redacted] tells me, tells the whole class: Oh, yeah, big bad Mister Teacher Man gonna kick my blackass out of class for talkin about Jesus now. That must make you feel like a big man, huh?

I'm not actually ready for him to actually step outside.

I'm ready for him to punch me in the face. Head butt me. Stomp all over me. Maybe pull a knife or a gun.

I'm trying not to come off as that scared-shitless-woke-in-theory-academic brand of racist.

I'm ready to explain the separation of church and state without infringing upon this freedom of religion.

You got a fuckin problem with me, bro?

Is everything okay? I say.

Yeah, I got a fuckin problem.

[Name Redacted] does not punch me or headbutt me or stomp all over me or pull a knife, but I can smell his sweet breath and feel his spit on my nose.

Listen, I have no problem with Jesus.

Listen, I like you, actually.
Listen, I'm just trying to help you.
It just seems like something larger is going on.
You goddamn right there's something larger going on, bro.

[Name Redacted] does not punch me or headbutt me or stomp all over me or pull a knife, but I can smell his sweet breath and feel his spit on my nose.

Maybe it would be better if we could discuss this with a counselor?

So you don't feel like I'm persecuting you?

Man, fuck this place. And fuck all y'all whiteassed racist motherfuckers.

He turns and heads back to the classroom.

He doesn't get on top of the desk and preach or start a protest.

He grabs his bible/zine and his bag and storms out.

I do not feel good about writing up a complaint about him to the student conduct board.

I do not feel good noting that I fear he might come back and incite violence.

They say that I did the right thing. They say I had no authority to kick him out of class unless I felt like he was an imminent threat to other students.

They don't say anything about an imminent threat to me, but I'm kind of glad for that.

I've seen *Dangerous Minds*.

I don't think of myself as a white savior or anything.

At least I don't like to think I think that.

Whatever impact I might have had on him, I'll never know.

I never see or hear from [Name Redacted] again.

But he was right.

I'm not fuckin Jesus.

If I were, I probably would've been able to get him to come back to my flock and work in groups on MLA in-text citations.

BARBIE

ALL I DO NOW IS WALK THE DOGS and listen to white-people podcasts.

This morning I see a Barbie doll tied up to the back of one of the campus golf carts. Its eyes blacked out.

Like some *True Detective* cult shit.

But even that I've seen before.

The dogs want to free it, to chew its head off, and rip off its dyed blond hair.

I do a loop hoping to see the grounds crew guy who drove the Barbie mobile.

I imagine giving an interview on *Dateline*.

Keith Morris: *Didn't it seem strange the doll wrapped in twine like that, its eyes blacked out?*

Me: *Nah, not really. Not around these parts. Not if you've seen what I've seen.*

I tell myself it's probably a joke, but I also take a bunch of photos and the whole time I'm waiting for some serial-killer looking dude to come out from the early morning shadows with a rag of chloroform.

I want to see if my dogs really would rip him from limb to limb or if they'd cower in the face of true evil.

The dogs do not like the golfcarts with leaf blowers.

Or the guys who drive the other golf carts and stop to change the garbages.

It gets awkward.

Most of them of the guys are black.

Half of them want to pet my dogs and tell me how beautiful their coats are, how strong their jaws must be.

Half of them would pour hot gravy on their paws if it'd encourage them to eat themselves from limb to limb.

There's little in-between in the looks they give me while reaching out to pet versus lunging backwards.

And I get it.

I tell them and tell them: They're all bark and no bite.

They're big cuddle bugs if you could see them at home.

But their barks and their lunging and their snarling and the teeth, in the dark, before the sun has risen, when evil lurks, it's not hard to imagine these trash dogs might've been fighting dogs in another life.

My one dog is a 100-pound mix between a rottweiler, doberman, and a german shepherd.

Every 80s-90's attack dog wrapped up in one.

And then the pitbull.

And then the boykin lab, who isn't scary, but he's bred to hunt and is the smarts of the operation.

I get them squeaky ducks and rabbits and beavers; they tear their heads off, rip their stuffing out. They eat their squeakers and shit them out whole.

This morning I listen to a podcast about a serial killer who buried murder kits all around the country.

Yeah? I am thinking, you should see the holes in my backyard.

And it's a real pain in the ass to clean up after their shit as well.

I'm thinking why would anybody ever listen to anything I had to tell them?

I'm thinking, I'm sorry.

I'm so so sorry.

For all of this.

And where did that Barbie doll go?

BURGER KING GUY: ACT I

DUDE SITTING ON THE BENCH at the softball fields this morning asks me if the men's room is open and then tells me it's not open.

I have the dogs with me but he doesn't seem scared.

Or off-put that I'm letting them drink straight from the drinking fountains. They have little censors like grocery doors and the dogs have pretty quickly figured them out: *We are genius dogs!*

The guy, this kid, he looks maybe 25, 26, dressed the kids dress these days. Not homeless chic but not all that well-homed chic either. Could be a 4.0 engineering major, could be a crazed homeless guy.

I choose to assume the former.

I say, Yeah, nah, they're real inconsistent with the men's room. The women's room stays unlocked a lot of the time, but men's you have to get lucky.

I don't say it's because it's the softball fields. The baseball field's on the other side of campus. But he's black and I don't want to whitesplain gender, sports, and public restrooms to him.

He says he doesn't have to go or anything, he just needs to get his stuff right.

He says he works at Burger King across the highway. (The highway? It's four-lanes and 35 mph in a town of 25 hundred).

I ask, Aren't they open? (It's 6:30 in the morning).

No, sir, they ain't open yet.

I don't ask why he doesn't want to get straight in the Dunkin Donuts' bathroom or the Hardee's bathroom or the Circle K bathroom or Food Lion bathroom or any of the other places that are open next to Burger King.

I don't want to think it's because drugs. He doesn't look like a drug guy. Whatever a drug guy looks like. Whatever this guy looks like.

He looks about six four, six five and swol (as the kids say these days). He looks like he could be on the football team or the basketball team, but his being a young black man, I try not to dwell too long about him looking like a stereotype.

Thank god the dogs are too happy drinking from the water fountains to growl or bark or lunge like they usually do at black people, especially black guys, young black guys.

I say, You know the ladies' is open, man. I'm not too proud to admit I've had to jump in there a few times for emergencies. Hell, if I hadn't already gone this morning, I'd—

I give him a wink: I won't tell if you won't.

Nah, sir, he says. I ain't tryin to have nobody catch me in no women's bathroom.

All the kids down here say yes sir no sir, but it's still messed up, having a young black man calling me yes sir and no sir all the time. I'm 45, but I'm not 55. And this ain't 1960.

I want to tell him to get over himself. That it's 6:30 and we're at the softball fields, and school's out for the summer, nobody's around to catch him in the ladies' room.

I want to tell him it's not about being gay or trans or anything, it's just practical. If you need the bathroom you need the bathroom (even if it's just to get straight).

But I don't.

I can see it in his eyes. I can see it in my eyes. This six-foot-four/-five swol black dude getting caught sneaking out of the softball players' bathroom by some campus police swinging dick.

I want to ask again about why he doesn't want to go in any of the bathrooms of all the other places that are open down the street from BK.

I know that answer but I still can't stop myself from wanting to ask.

Well, shit, man, I'm sorry, I say, pulling the dogs away. That's shitty.

The dogs whine to get up closer to him, but don't growl or act like they're going to tear him limb from limb the way they do with a lot of black guys (it's pretty fucked up actually).

They cool? the guy asks, deciding if he wants to put his hand out to be sniffed and licked or not.

Yeah, I say. They just want to jump on you and lick you to death.

I immediately regret saying that.

But he puts his hand out anyway and they whine and lick him and even though I have to pull them to keep them from jumping up on him, he doesn't pull back or anything.

So there, I think. Maybe there's hope for us yet.

I look at my watch, it's quarter til now. Well, bud, I say, pulling my dogs away. I don't know what to tell you. At least you don't have much longer to get straight before work.

Yes, sir, he says. I mean no sir. I mean thank you.

He reaches out to shake my hand but by that time the dogs are already mushing me back towards home.

Fucking Burger King, I'm thinking to myself. How are you gonna compete with McDonalds and Hardees and Dunkin Donuts if you don't open up until goddamn 7 in the morning.

Or maybe they're on the way to closing for good.

Or maybe it's just a small-town thing, a southern thing.

Or maybe he had it wrong all along — on purpose or by mistake.

Whatever it is I'm making real judgements about work ethic until I go back to my podcast about true crime.

KEVIN

KEVIN SAYS SIEGFRIED AND ROY HAD IT COMING.
He means Roy, specifically, had it coming, and by *coming* he means Roy almost getting his throat ripped out by his 600-pound pet white tiger Mantacore.

But then there are probably lots of Roys who had it coming and we all know when you're talking about Siegfried and Roy having it coming you really mean Roy had it coming.

Kevin's half-drunk off Scotch because he's that kind of drinker. He's the kind of drinker who brings his own flask of Scotch to a party so he knows he's gonna be drinking the right kind of Scotch.

It's not much of a party—just me, my future ex-wife, Kevin, and Kevin's future ex-wife.

Against my wishes, my future ex-wife has convinced me to heavily sedate all the dogs and leave them locked up in the bedroom for the night, so as not to have our pets try to rip Kevin's or Kevin's pregnant wife's throat out.

It's probably for the best. It's no fun for anybody when you have a black friend over and all three of your dogs—the pitbull, the rottweiler, or the hunting breed—won't stop barking and growling at the one black person versus the three white people of similar age and social status.

There's only so many times you can say, Oh they're all just a bunch of a Teddy bears. They're all bark, no bite. They just love to play so much. They just take a little getting warmed up, a little calmed down. Sometimes they're just a little apprehensive around men. The three different places we rescued them from all said they were abused as puppies.

You leave out the part where the rescue lady is Southern and white with complicated views on animals v humans, makes sure to tell you that it was some black guy in each case.

You know how it is, she says, probably training him to be a fight dog, she says. Like that [expletive] Mike Vick.

Rescuing dogs is complicated in Southernass Georgia. There's the race thing. The socioeconomics of dog abuse. There's how many black kids have been attacked by pitbulls, rottweilers, german shepherds, dobermans, and assorted hunting dogs.

And all those violent dogs then put to death for the sole reason of all the abuse they were born into.

Between the three of our mutts, we tick off all the most banned dog breeds and though they've never actually attacked anybody or anything, they are a combined 275 pounds of muscle, bark, teeth, and growl whenever people ring the doorbell or knock on the door or try to pet them when I walk them as the mythical Cerberus, the protectorate of Southeast Georgia.

Which is that much more of a thing when it's a black guy knocking on the door and in your house and saying things about racism with increasing volume and hand gestures.

It's not like the North where you turn up your nose and tell people you rescued your dog and they pat you on the back and then go on a diatribe about the way some people treat their dogs.

Some people. Those people. You people.

White people.

It's always the people that's the problem.

Guns don't kill people, people you disagree with kill people. Animals kill people who don't like animals.

But back to Kevin and Roy and Siegfried and white tigers.

I don't disagree with Kevin but it's not like the tiger killed Roy and it's too easy to make jokes about sexually ambiguous lion/tiger tamers.

We might as well start taking pot shots at Steve Irwin. Why don't we all start piling on Grizzly Man while we're at it.

We all have it coming, I announce to the group. The real question is what they'll write on your Facebook page in memoriam.

Nobody nods or chuckles. Including not Kevin.

White people..., Kevin mutters.

Kevin being the only black friend my wife or I know at this point. *Friend* maybe a strong word.

We're both writers and teach college in Southernass Georgia so we should really at least have more black acquaintances that we are friendly with.

We try to make up for our lack of black friends by donating to NAACP and other black causes but it's not the same thing.

The answer to the question of why we don't have more black friends is the question: How many black guys want to teach at a college in Southernass Redneck County, Georgia, where they're still pissed off at Sherman's little march to the sea?

Kevin teaches sociology.

That means Kevin gets to teach a bunch of frat bros and sorority girls about the relationship between socioeconomics, education, crime, violence, abuse, and institutional racism in America. He gets to talk about fun things like generational trauma.

Kevin has made it pretty clear that the only reason he's living and working here is because he's actually from here. And now he's gonna have a kid, which means he wants to be close to his family.

Which means taking a job at Southernass Redneck University to teach a bunch of young Republicans about institutional racism in America.

You people..., Kevin says, shaking his head with a wry smile. At least it's not a withering stare. I've gotten the withering stare before. It makes me question a lot of decisions I've made to get me here.

Like me my future ex-wife is a Northerner, a Yankee (which is weird to be called when you are from Northernass Wisconsin, but that's life in Southernass Georgia).

Like me, she is white—as in: *real* white, German and Scandinavian white—so for all intents and purposes we are *You people*.

And so is Kevin's future ex-wife.

Sarah.

Sarah from Kansas seeming even whiter than us somehow. Despite her teaching African American literature, specializing in Ralph Ellison and *The Invisible Man*.

Sarah is six months pregnant with Kevin's baby.

Sarah, earlier in the night, making the mistake of telling us about how she'd done one of those 23 and Me's.

I'd just like to have a clear idea of what all I'm passing down to little Kevin Jr., she says touching her belly with her wine glass.

How much wine is okay during pregnancy? I'm not going to ask.

And anyway, this is the part where the person tells you that they have something like .0001 percent Native American or Southeast Asian in them. Maybe some distant Māori thrown in there. Anything to make them less white.

Sarah is 100% honky.

Same way I'm 100% honky. And my wife is 100% honky.

We're all joking and laughing about it, which is how I end up getting too comfortable and making the mistake of asking—jokingly—what Kevin is.

You people, Kevin says. To me and his own wife.

You people.

Kevin doesn't say anything about me wearing my Biggie *Ready to Die* t-shirt. And if that makes me less or more *you people*. In retrospect, I imagine my Biggie shirt being akin to wearing a band's shirt to their own concert.

One of those people.

No, I didn't do no fuckin ancestry test, Kevin says. What's a motherfuckin ancestry test gonna tell me I don't already know?

He then goes into all the things an ancestry test would probably tell him about his slave ancestors and it's not something you would probably want to know more about if you were a black sociology professor like Kevin. At least not something that's going to liven up a party with a bunch of whiteass people.

We all—me, my future ex-wife, and Kevin's future ex-wife—laugh awkwardly like he's Dave Chappelle or Chris Rock and we've paid to see the show and opened ourselves up to be heckled for our absurd privilege and dorky mannerisms.

You people, Kevin mumbles again and then heads out to smoke a swisher sweet.

Pretty quickly I follow after him like a puppy following its abusive owner.

Partially because I want to show that I can take a little friendly ribbing about my whiteness, but also because my future ex-wife is soon to be my current ex-wife and because Sarah's at that stage of pregnancy where all she wants to talk about is being pregnant.

If I were back in college this is where I'd ask Kevin about his favorite rap albums growing up. I'd drop names like Eric B. And Rakim. Slick Rick. Kool Keith. MF Doom.

Deep cuts. At least for white boys like me.

I'd debate him on how necessary Easy E was to NWA or Flavor Flav to Public Enemy.

I might slip in the fact that I used to teach a class on Harlem Renaissance and the History of Hip Hop for Upward Bound kids from inner city Milwaukee. Leaving out the fact that I only taught it once and all the kids wanted to do was write raps about anything that rhymes with money, cash, hoes—even the girls.

I know enough not to bring up basketball unless he brings it up first. I'm not going to slip in the fact that I used to play and then coach college basketball and most of the guys were black including my friend and roommate Q.

Or how one of the players was Terry Cummings' kid. Leaving out the fact that I was really just a glorified ball boy/practice team scrub and that Terry Cummings' kid hated me and once nearly knocked out my eyeball with an elbow accidentally on purpose after I'd made a couple threes, got too caught up in trash talk, and asked who his daddy was.

As a white boy, I really should've known better to question a black man's patrimony and it's one of the things I've most regretted saying to a black person over the years of my interactions with black people.

Thankfully, Kevin breaks the silence. What's up brother? he says and offers me a pull of his flask. It makes me so happy that I immediately forget about all the *you peoples*.

It's dark out and quiet, an intermittent stream of cars driving by. We live on the corner of one of those cut-through streets, so people are always either running the stop sign or idling at the stop sign to text, check Google Maps, and deposit their trash in our front yard.

I say, Yo. Thanks man. I don't call him brother. I don't call him dog or *dawg*. Though I used to call Q that when we roomed together. When I wasn't calling him Q and he wasn't calling me B. Though I'd never earned the right to be called *a brother from another mother*.

The rules for college ball and being a college professor are very different.

Kevin offers me a swisher sweet, I beg off. Nah man, I'm straight.

Do I tell him that I've never smoked anything in my life? No cigarettes, no weed, no crack, no swisher sweets?

No, no I don't.

He still hasn't mentioned anything about my Biggie shirt.

Fucking Sarah, right? he says. All this 23 and Me bullshit.

Like people are gonna be treating my shorty like some Scandinavian prince or something. Fuckin people.

This is one of those tricky ones where you're not sure if the guy wants you to take sides or just to listen to him vent.

Yeah, what a bitch, can backfire on you pretty quickly.

I say, Yeah, man. I feel ya. Then wait for him to call me on it and ask what I can actually feel for him.

Mercifully, he doesn't.

This is their first year here and my future ex-wife had said we should have them over. It's hard enough being new down here, she'd said.

I'm not sure if the insinuation was *hard enough without being pregnant* or *hard enough without being black* or *hard enough without being a black man with a pregnant white wife*.

I'm gonna go ahead and select all of the above.

Fuckin 23 and Me, that shit's fucked from the jump, yo.

I am both proud and ashamed of my codeswitching game. It can be quite conflicting being the honky all the time.

Right? he says. Right? That's what I'm talking about, dude. He gives me a fist bump with his swisher sweet hand and offers me another pull off his flask with his other.

Nah, nah, I'm straight I say, thinking how much does a flask hold anyway and if he's had to refill off our non-bourbon whiskey. Not that there'd be anything wrong with that.

More like I wish I just knew what kind of bourbon he drank so I could proudly offer him some first thing in the door. Hold up some Johnny Blue. Hey, check out this shit out, yo. I gotcha covered, bro.

You know what I wouldn't offer him? Not Remy Martin. Not Cristal. Definitely not that Henny.

In my head, all I can think of is every story about me interacting with a black person in my life so I can establish my black-guy street cred. Show him I'm not like all the other *white people* who teach at the college.

I settle on asking him about what it was like growing up around here, but I don't get to it.

I don't get to it because that's when some kid blaring loud shitty music in a Lexus swerves to avoid t-boning this old black lady Miss Deva from up the street in her boat of a Caddy.

Miss Deva (her actual name), she doesn't even look back, just keeps on driving as if nothing happened, which probably I would too if I was an old black lady surely to get blamed for causing a white kid in a Lexus to wreck.

Miss Deva making a living by giving readings, probably she'd done read her own reading and headed straight home.

Meanwhile the Lexus skips over the sidewalk, clocks a telephone or power pole and ends up skidding into our front yard, almost into our bedroom with sweet innocent heavily sedated three monsters snoring away.

Holy fucking shit, I say.

Well fuck me, Kevin says. Takes one last hit off his swisher and a pull off his scotch. Puts them down and strides over like he's seen this happen a hundred times.

Maybe he has. I don't know. Is it racist to assume that maybe Kevin grew up in a neighborhood where people were crashing into front yards with some consistency?

I find out later that he put himself through college as an EMT.

But I only find this out after the fact.

In the heat of it, I'm kind of pissed that he's beating me to the punch. Does the white savior complex cover trying to save other white people before other black people can save them?

I'm know down deep I am not a good person. And constantly being aware that I'm not a good person and thinking not-good thoughts makes it worse in my mind. Maybe other minds as well, other minds such as my future ex-wife's mind.

Kevin's over to the driver's side pulling the kid out of the front seat and gently laying him down on the grass. Kevin holding the kid's hand and asking questions before I even get down the steps off the front porch.

Better have someone call 911, Kevin hollers as he kneels next to the kid.

How bad is it? I say.

Just call 911, Kevin says.

I don't have my phone on me, the way I never seem to be prepared to be the hero of anything.

I don't say that though. I just holler at Sarah to call. I'm not about to be hollering at my future ex-wife to be doing anything I demand of her.

They're both out on the porch watching now. Both still with their drinks in their hands.

What happened? Sarah asks.

Are they gonna be okay? my wife asks.

He's gonna be fine, I say.

Be careful, my wife says. (It almost breaks my heart to hear she still cares.)

Be careful, Kevin says. I feel less emotional support from him. More like sincere skepticism.

The car is still running. The radio still blaring some EDM glow-stick rave shit, that has now become the soundtrack to the entire to the show.

A telephone or power pole is lying on top of the smashed windshield. The front end including the bumper completely U'ed from impact.

Wires everywhere.

I start thinking of every action movie or TV show I've ever seen where something sparks and the car explodes five feet in the air and kills everyone close—except for the main character.

Am I the main character here? A question for history to answer.

I should be asking Kevin what to do but my pride won't let me ask him what to do.

Watch out, my wife hollers at me. There's electrical wires everywhere.

Nothing to worry about, I say. I'll be fine. What I mean is: if Kevin's fine, then why is everybody worried about me being fine?

Kevin hollers for a first-aid kid. He means the first-aid kit I should've run for immediately after Kevin beat me to running to pull the kid out of the car.

And now my wife is beating me to that punch as well.

Sarah hollers at me what our address is. I start stuttering, my mind going blank. My wife beats me to that punch as well. Hollers it out from all the way in the bathroom.

Where am I?

I'm standing there frozen in front of the wires and the car still running and thinking that should be me over there holding the kid's hand and calming him down. It's my goddamn front yard.

I had to be CPR certified back when I was coaching in college. That was one class and it was 20 years ago now, but still, I should be able to do something other than stand here.

Fifteen and two. That's what I remember. Chest thrusts, breaths. One or the other. Clear the airways. Don't move the neck if you don't have to. Just like riding a bike, I'm telling myself.

Anybody called 911? Kevin hollers.

I'm talking to them right now, Sarah yells.

Where's that first-aid kit? Kevin hollers.

We're on it, I say. Emphasis on *we're*.

How's he doing? I say.

I'm trying to see through from the other side of the car. I can see Kevin but not the kid.

Kevin, he says.

Kevin?

Kevin says Kevin's going to be okay but he's got a nasty cut on his head.

I go silent for what seems like five minutes trying and then eventually understanding that Kevin isn't talking about himself in the third person the way rappers and basketball players do. It's called illeism. I looked it up once for something to bring up and make lame jokes about at just such a party. *Yo, that's Ill-eism.* Did you hear what Nas should'a called his album before *Illmatic*? *Illeismatic, yo.* Or: *Yo, you know that Jay-Z has referred to himself in the third-person over 786 times on his albums?*

The kid's name is Kevin, too. Which is fucking unnecessarily confusing.

I'm staring at the wires all around the car and then the car still running, the radio still bumping, and once again thinking about every time I've seen a car blow up on TV.

Cars don't blow up like that in real life. That's what they all say.

That's what they all say until one day it really happens.

Shouldn't we get him away from the car before it blows? I holler over the thumping baseline.

Nah, nothing's gonna blow and Kevin needs to stay as still as possible. I just need you to turn off the car for me.

I stand there still.

It's just TV cables, he says. There's nothing electric to shock you.

Which becomes obvious as soon as he says it. They're fucking TV cables. There's no power cables. No telephone cables.

My wife is already running over to Kevin with the first-aid kit and I haven't moved five feet.

I am no white savior. I can't even save white people.

White people... I can hear Kevin muttering that as he watches me stand there frozen. I can't actually hear him. The car running, the music bumping. But I can imagine him muttering it. *Fucking white people.*

Sarah is now out there next to me. She's still on the phone. *Is he still conscious, baby?* she hollers.

It's the first time I've heard her call Kevin baby. Or anything else than Kevin, or Kev-in or K'vn!

He's good, baby, Kevin says. We're just breathin over here, baby. Just chillin and chattin, aren't we Kev? Just a little cut on his head. A little shook up, nothin big.

Goddamn Kevin and his smoothness. Always with his smoothness.

I still haven't turned off the car. Haven't shut off the teeth-rattling music. In lieu of not yet having turned off the car, I holler, What about a concussion? Is he dizzy or having a headache?

The neighbors are out now. Most of them 80 years old in their sleep clothes, whether that's a nightgown or tank top and boxers. All of them white. And so that's embarrassing me now too—how white a neighborhood we live in.

Where's Miss Deva when you fucking need her?

Some neighbors planted firmly in their driveways gawking. A couple of them inching in closer without being prompted by me or Kevin. Nobody's hollered out: *It's just TV cables, nothing electric.* Nobody's hollered out, *Nothing to see here. Just a little accident.*

One of the closer ones in a nightgown asks me if we need her to call 911.

No thanks, Sarah says with the phone to her chest, I'm talking to them right now. Cops are on their way.

The crowd is here watching us perform our roles and I can't even be the communication director. Cars are driving by slowly but not that slowly. Veering in scarily as they gawk on by.

Can somebody get this goddamn noise turned off?

The music has almost become white noise at this point. Like I said, the soundtrack to the whole shitty EDM scene.

My sooner-to-be ex-wife is over there waiting on Kevin like she's his Julianna Margulies to his *ER*-era George Clooney.

I got it, I blurt out finally.

No, I'm here already, she says.

There's no *baby* in there. No *honey*. Not even a *Benji,* which I hate, but I'd've taken at that point.

She's doing. Not talking. Not thinking.

Fuckin christ, Kevin hollers as a car comes speeding by. Can somebody get out there and direct traffic til the cops get here?

I got it, I blurt out finally. I got it.

It's dark out and I'm wearing a black Biggie t-shirt and dark blue jeans. I don't have a flashlight or even my phone.

I'm just running madly out to the intersection to wave my arms and shout and, if need be, take a charge or two.

Nobody says anything about the dangerous nature of this. Or the courage to undertake it for the safety of all.

I'd once gotten drunk after a bad practice in college—by bad practice, I mean the best player on the team, the son of Terry Cummings, who was very black, had called me a shit-eating little *w-n-word* and whipped a basketball at the back of my head—which had led me to the getting drunk and deciding to walk across a bridge at two in the morning and put my life in fate's hands: if I'm meant to keep on being a shit-eating little w-n-word I'll make it all the way without a scratch. If I'm meant to sacrifice myself to make the world better for non-shit-eating *w-n-word*s, then I'll take one for the team.

And here I was back out there taking on on-coming traffic as proof that I had not learned my lesson or that God or the World or Karma had had second thoughts about me.

Immediately, upon assuming my position as protector, two cop cars come flying in with their lights on and sirens and then horns honking for me to get the fuck out of the way.

What the fuck are you doing, bro? Kevin hollers.

Get the fuck out of the road, my future ex-wife hollers.

I'm fine, I say. I'm fine. Somebody needs to step up.

And that somebody is gonna be me.

Even that rings on deaf ears. The cops on the scene asking their questions. Shining their flashlights. Talking on their talkies.

Get this guy out of the road! Nobody hollering that. They were definitely not hollering *Give this guy the medal of valor* or *Buy this guy a beer for bravery*.

Me standing there like an idiot in the middle of the road watching everything. Kevin still holding the guy's hand, my future-ex-wife holding a bloodstained towel to Kevin's head. Other Kevin.

Other Kevin looking like he's 12 years old. This pudgy punk kid. His hair dyed blue. A wife-tank top with the misogynistic name, a flame-patterned skater shorts down his ass, black socks up to his knees. A nose ring shining in the light.

Everything the opposite of Kevin. Probably one of those electronica-pop punks who secretly throws the n-word around to impress his pop punk friends who secretly hate black guys for being cooler, rappers and jocks, and for not being into electronica-pop punk. Not getting *The Movement*. For laughing at them every time they'd cruise their daddy's Lexus through the hood, dismissing them as the trust-fund nepo-babies they were.

And yet here's Kevin holding his hand and asking him about his band and his mom, whatever the shit he's asking, I can't here.

But it's clear there's no *White people...* No *You people...* No eye-rolling consternation of a lifetime of micro-aggressions.

It's *buddy* and *bro* and *Kev* and *K-money*.

It kind of pisses me off to be honest.

How long do I hear the sirens, the honking for before I turn to face my fate.

The ambulance nearly mowing me down before swerving at the last very second. *What the f—?* I yell as it skims past.

I even slap it and very nearly take off my arm as it careens into the ditch heading straight for Kevin, Kevin, my future-ex-wife, and two cops.

It doesn't take them out. It only almost takes them out in such a way as to make everybody blame me.

What the fuck, dude?

Get the fuck out of the road, man?

Benjamin Karl Drevlow! —my future ex-wife.

Even my name is an embarrassment to me tonight. How white it is. It's German and Scandinavian roots. *Like people are gonna treat my kid like some Scandinavian prince,* Kevin had said.

I'm not feeling much like a Scandinavian prince or German prince.

Who am I saving? From whom?

What I do, I listen. I decide to become an ally. I get the fuck out of the road. Let the cops and ambulance do their thing. Let Kevin direct them the whole time.

I sulk. I skulk. Back inside and make myself a whiskey drink. Jack and Coke. It ain't Remy or Henny or Cristal but it's enough to get me drunk.

I mumble to myself. Replay the lines: *Get out the road! What the fuck are you doing? What were you thinking? Benjamin Karl Drevlow!*

I let my three dogs, still mostly stoned, out of the bedroom. I put some old Johnny Cash on the turntable. Turn it up.
I shot a man in Reno just to watch him die.
The original gangsta rapper.
Even if he'd never actually shot a man in Reno.

I wrote a paper in college once about persona poems. I compared Robert Browning's Porphyria's Lover to about eight Eminem songs about murdering his ex-wife Kim. I made the case that they were essentially the same thing.

My teacher, a very white very old woman, gave me an A. She said she'd never thought about it that way. But very much agreed with me.

This being pre-Me-Too.

I had my wife read it once, hoping she'd give me an A, too. Wanting her to see that there was an art to be made in portrayal of the violence towards women that rappers often played out under their rap personas.

This is you trying to excuse Eminem's misogyny? she said. Comparing him to Porphyria's Lover? This is you saying, Well, if some old white guy from the late 1800's writes about murdering his lover, then it must be okay for Eminem to do it now?

I remember thinking, Well, if Dr. Sutton thought it was an A...? And she was a hard-core feminist from back in the sixties.

I remember thinking this and not saying it and now being happy that I'd thought something and for once hadn't say it and how maybe if I did that more often, I'd be wrong less often. At least with my future ex-wife.

It's an hour before Sarah comes back in. An hour and a half before my future ex-wife. Closer to two hours before Kevin.

Me sitting on the floor back against armchair with one hand alternating petting three stoned monsters and the other gripping a big-gulp glass full of Jack and Coke. The caffeine jittering my nerves, the Jack making everything around me slow and unsteady.

Fucking white people, Kevin says immediately upon entering.

The dogs don't even bark. Barely register his existence with a whine.

Right? my wife says.

If they're waiting for me to ask for context I'm not going to bite. Neither are the dogs.

What? Sarah says.

These fucking cops, my wife says. All they want to know is what the old woman was driving. Did we get her license plate? Did we get a good look at her face? Did we recognize her from the neighborhood?

Fucking cops, Kevin says. He takes a swig off his flask and then tips it up and shakes it. Not a drop left.

Hey bro, you mind? he says to me holding up the bottle of Jack.

Oh yeah, help yourself, my wife says.

Did you see what happened? Sarah asks Kevin.

Yeah, he says. Some fucking little punk probably changing tunes on his iPhone nearly t-bones some sweet old black lady just minding her own business.

There's no Kev anymore. No K-money. No holding anybody's hand and telling them it's gonna be okay.

Meanwhile they don't say shit about little Kevin's weed, my wife says.

Weed? Sarah says.

You couldn't smell it? my wife says.

My man, Kev, he was groovin on some funky herb most def.

It's my turn now. It's one of those tricky things, putting yourself back into a conversation after you've been listening and stewing too long. The right tone. No blurting. No stuttering. No coming in hot. No coming in cold.

Still, I say. Miss Deva could've at least come back and checked on him. Shit, I mean he could've been dead for all she knew.

Miss Deva? Kevin says and right away I realize I've come in too hot.

Who the fuck's this Miss Deva? he says again. Miss fuckin Deva?

Miss Deva? my wife says.

Who's Miss Deva? Sarah says.

All eyes on me.

Them all standing around the kitchen still coming down from the night's events, me sitting in a recliner sipping my liquor and stroking the back of the dogs' heads like Grandpa just having finished the old ball game, the homers having lost in a blowout.

Miss Deva, I say to my wife. Over on College. College and third. The one with the readings.

Miss Deva? she says. That was her. You saw?

Sometimes I like to help her out, I say. Let her do my reading. Give her a little something extra. She comes around with her fliers sometimes.

Missus fucking Deva, Kevin says. She give you a good reading, bro? What'd she say about tonight?

Nah, I say. It ain't like that. I don't go for that shit. I just try to be nice.

Oh, you don't go for that shit, huh, bro?

So you didn't stick around to say something? my wife says.

What's it gonna do, me ratting out some old poor black lady? I say. It's not like Kev died or anything. He's just a little cut, right?

Oh he's got a cut, all right, Kevin says. Kevin's sat down on the couch now. He has the whole bottle of Jack and he's taking long hard pulls off it. Ol' Kev gonna have some splainin to do when he get to the hospital. All that herb on him.

And fuckin Miss Deva, he says again as if the name itself is somehow an affront to him.

It's a thing I've had to get accustomed to down here—calling old people by their first name. Miss Deva. Miss Rhonda. Mister Ben. Christ, now that got complicated. These 18-year-old kids calling me Mister Ben, Mister Ben. These 18-year-old black kids calling me Mister Ben, Mister Ben.

That thick southern accent, sometimes it starting to sound like Master Ben, Master Ben... Talk about a headfuck.

No thanks, you can just call me... What the fuck should I be telling them, 18-year-old black girls and guys what they should call me.

I'm not saying that, I say. I'm not saying she should've come back and turned herself in or anything. I'm just saying.

Oh you're just saying, Kevin says.

Meanwhile little punkass Kev saying over and over how it wasn't his fault. Fuckin old bitch turns her turning signal on doesn't turn. *What'd she look like?* The old bitch she looked like I don't know... Black, he says, Kevin says. He's lit up a swisher sweet in the house, which isn't cool, but it's been a night, so okay, it's cool.

It ain't my fault, it ain't my fault, Kevin sing-songs. Fuckin white people...

Do you think they'll bust him? Sarah says. Sarah's done drinking wine now. Sitting on the arm of the couch next to Kevin, one arm around him, one arm resting on her unborn baby.

You think they'll bust him? Kevin says and rolls his eyes.
Yeah?

For what? For being white? For his parents buying him a Lexus? For his blaming an old black lady just a minding her business? Just what do you think these fuckin pigs gonna bust poor little Kevin's ass for?

That's fucked up, my future ex-wife says. It's true, but it's fucked up.

Good old Miss Deva, Kevin says. Ain't that right, bro?

I mean, I don't know, I say. It was dark out. I wasn't looking that closely. Maybe... I mean I'm just saying.

You're just sayin.

I mean, I'm just sayin the whole thing was kinda fucked.

Fucked is right, man, Kevin says. He's not nodding at me, not raising a drink to me, not putting out a fist to be bumped.

I'm doing my best to focus on petting the dogs without actually arousing them and not making eye contact with anybody. My big black rottweiler-german shepherd rescue reformed fighting dog whimpering a little in his dreams, whatever sad dream he might be dreaming.

Just imagine, my future ex-wife says trailing off. Then: What a shit show. She's coming over to sit on the couch next to Kevin. She's handing him a lowball glass, ice half melted, a little cherry in the bottom. Kevin's pouring her a shot of Jack. He's not even looking. He's looking out the window. At nothing but darkness and one dim streetlight. The cherries and berries long gone.

Just imagine, my future ex-wife says again. She looks at me and then back at Kevin. Just imagine if it weren't for... she says and trails off.

I'm just saying, I say one more time. I'm just saying the whole thing was...

I look at Kevin. I can't draw his eyes. He's staring out the window. Sarah staring at him, leaning on him.

I look at my wife. And she's not looking at me. She's not patting Kevin on the thigh or anything—the hero's pat. But her hand's over there. It might be all the Jack and Coke, but her fingers look to me to be inching closer and closer, and further and further away at the same time.

Welp, I say, holding my big gulp glass up for everybody to say. Here's to fucking Miss Deva getting away scott free, I say. I let out a little drunken giggle. Trying to lighten up the room.

Nobody responds.

I'm about to say, Well, then here's to fucking punkass Kev for getting away with it.

I don't get to say it though.

It's Kevin. He nearly jumps up off the couch. Throws off Sarah's arm over his shoulders. Tells Sarah it's time to get out of these people's home.

She says yeah. And then apologizes for staying too long.

Sarah says it's been a long night. Sarah says we should do this again sometime. Hopefully less drama next time. She thanks us for inviting them over.

Kevin apologizes too. He apologizes to nobody in particular, puts the Jack back in the kitchen and then heads for the door. Just before he leaves though, he puts a fist up, like the black power fist, he doesn't turn back, just holds it there, lets the door close on it. It's been real people, he hollers over his shoulder, the pulls the door shut behind him, nearly catches Sarah in the process.

My wife spends the rest of the night replaying everything Kevin had done and said and asking if I heard that or if I remember this.

Miss Deva, she says. Really? Are you sure?

Just imagine, she says that too. Just imagine if...

I just nod and say mm-hmm, sit there on the floor in front of my recliner, pet the dogs and watch them drool on the carpet. I know, right?

She never once says, Well, you too, baby. You were there, and you did things, too. You nearly got yourself runover. You were the true hero.

Nobody ever does come back to clean up the broken glass and trash that had spewed out of Kev's Lexus. The four big ruts cut into our lawn from the Lexus and the ambulance.

No, that's all left to me.

Did I have this all coming to me all along? Did I deserve what I got? Did I believe that I was a good person trying to do good things and that good things would come to good people?

No, no I do not.

But then this story is not really about me I guess.

MJ

THIS MORNING I DREAM I'm trying to tell my ex-wife which flavor of Gatorade I want.

I don't drink Gatorade.

My ex-wife doesn't do my shopping anymore now that she's my ex-wife.

Last week I had a dream where my dog kept lapping up my bowl of soup from my lap and I couldn't make him stop.

I can't shout.

I can't talk.

I can't move my arms.

I don't eat soup.

Most dreams I have are dreams where I can't talk or move my legs or my arms.

It's always a little disconcerting but at this point my dreaming mind mostly takes sleep paralysis in stride.

Mmmmm-mmmm-mmmm-mmmm-muhhhhhh.

That's the way I talk in my dreams.

I once had a dream where all my students formed a mob with sharpened #2 pencils and stormed my bedroom to demand A's for their broken sonnets.

It was evals day.

Mmmmmmm-mmmmm-mmmm-muhhhh, I try to tell them.

It's unclear if they can't hear me, don't understand me, or just ignore me.

Ever have the dream where the people you work with ignore you/can't hear you and you end up screaming in their faces and they still ignore you/can't hear you until you wake up out of breath?

Say Mmmmmmmmm-mmmm-muh, if you agree.

None of my dreams are very interesting.

None of them mean anything all that deep or revelatory.

I don't even remember most of my dreams.

Except for that one time a year where I have the jumping dream.

Where I can move my arms and legs.

But more than that I can dunk a basketball.

In the dream it's easy. Like breathing or talking with lips that will work.

A 45-year-old, 300-pound, five-eleven white guy who can dunk it like Jordan flying in from the free-throw line.

And sometimes it'll go so far as I can just jump and jump and fly through the air, bounding over buildings and rivers and lakes and hills and valleys and so many people too small to see me soaring above them as I palm the basketball in one hand searching searching for my slam-dunk championship backboard to smash.

It's not a superhero thing.

It's not a flying thing.

It's a jumping thing.

Like imagine Jordan flying in from the free-throw line but times a thousand.

Like imagine if that Gatorade song came true:

Sometimes I dream /

that he is me /

I wanna [fly through the air and dunk the basketball from way behind free-throw line…] like Mike. /

I wannabe wanna be wanna be /

Like Mike. /

I want to be like Mike.

I don't know what this all means and I don't want to know what this all means.

It's just the only dream I ever remember that I want to come true.

That feels so true.

So true that I sometimes have to remind myself that I can't dunk a basketball.

I never have sex dreams.

My ex-wife no longer takes my calls.

And I don't even like Gatorade.

Mmmmm-mmmmm-mmmmm-muhhhhh.

That's the sound of me dying an invalid.

Having lost my limbs to diabetes.

Having lost the art of the spoken word.

My sixth heart attack, my fourth stroke, my third aneurysm.

Please Nurse Ratchet, I'm begging you, smother me now, I've got no love left to give.

Mmmmm-mmmmm-mmmmm-muhhhhh.

BURGER KING GUY: ACT II

GODDAMNIT, I'VE GONE AND DONE IT AGAIN.
Offered this homeless guy 20 bucks for food, drink, drugs, whatever, I don't care.
This is not a humble brag.
This is a real problem.
Not the drinking or drugs part.
The problem being that he's black—still black. I'm white—still white. And he isn't actually homeless—still not homeless.
As in: not since the last time I mistook him for maybe homeless.
Yo, I'm the manager of fucking Burger King, man, he says.
...Don't you remember me?
...I have an apartment.
...You see my watch? (It's gold, i.e. nicer than anything I accessorize.)
...See my kicks? (They're retro Jordan's. I had the original Jordan's when I was a kid, but still, his point is taken).
...I'm just fuckin hungover, dude.
He's been sleeping at a picnic table behind the library.
It's 7 on a Sunday morning, me out walking the dogs again.
I wonder how much of the awkwardness could've been assuaged if he'd known the lyrics to Sunday Comin Down by Kris Kristofferson. If we could've had a debate about who sang it better Kristofferson or Cash, which then could've maybe led to a discussion of Me and Bobby McGee by Kristofferson but sung by Janis Joplin and that line *Freedom's just another word for nothing left to lose.*

Shit, that's a good line, we could've both said and nodded and then had a moment of contemplation.
Oh shit, I say. Oh man I'm sorry.
I have to keep stopping myself from calling him brother.

Nah man, it's all right, he says handing my 20 dollars back. I'm just sick of this profiling shit. I'm holdin, know what I mean. I'm mother fuckin holdin.

For a second I think he means that he's *holdin* a gun and might try to use it on me.

Then I feel even shittier than I already am for assuming he was going to shoot me.

Whereas I'm now realizing that he means he's *holdin* money and possessions and… not homeless. As in: Not in need handouts from white peckerwood wannabe saviors like me.

Thankfully the dogs are in the back of my car.

These situations get even trickier when three barking, sometimes-growling rescue mutts are involved.

I can hear them barking and growling from my car and I try to ignore them. I try to think of all the half-legitimate excuses for why I didn't remember this dude and why I've once again assumed he was homeless.

I point at a beat-up tent tucked away in the woods behind the library, a pile of somebody's belongings.

Sorry, I say again, I just saw the tent and everything.

Ah shit, man, he says. You see? I didn't even notice that.

This seems to ease the tension of him thinking I've racially profiled him for being hungover in public. Once again.

I've been hungover in public many times. I've never been offered money for a hot meal.

We're both looking at the tent and the pile of things and I squint and think I can see a guy lying there.

Which then I'm like, shit, now I'm talking about a homeless dude like he's invisible.

Which is the real problem, isn't it?

We want to pretend they aren't even there.

Also, it turns out that the sleeping guy is black too. I'm realizing that as we're looking at him and talking about the problem with homelessness in this place.

Burger King guy says this is the worst homeless problem he's ever seen. He'd grown up in New Orleans and lived in Atlanta.

I find that very hard to believe. But then I've never lived in New Orleans or Atlanta and as has been established I'm probably not the best judge of homelessness problems.

Yeah, I say. It's rough around here.

Shit, man, I mean I didn't even notice that, Burger King guy says again pointing at the tent and the stuff and the black guy sleeping there.

The homeless problem. What does that really mean? *The most homeless place? The most depressing homeless place? The most violent? The craziest?*

All those statistics about mental illness and homeless.

My mom grew up in a small town in Minnesota that just happened to have the biggest mental institution in the state.

She used to tell me about how every Saturday morning, they'd open the doors and let the parade begin.

Oh they were mostly harmless, she'd say.

And the looks on their faces, they were so ecstatic to be able to go to the gas station/post office/general store for candy and cigarettes and hats and shirts and sweatshirts with the town's name and tourist slogans on them.

It was about the most exciting thing that ever happened in that town.

I'm not entirely sure about the ethics of entertaining yourself with a parade of the mentally ill. I've heard the stories about the way they treated the mentally ill back in those days. Those stories of course didn't include the stories of Saturday morning parades.

Who am I to judge?

Mister Good Samaritan giving money to the poor and the not-poor managers of Burger King.

The other thing that's become clear to me this morning is that not only have I seen Burger King guy before, I've also seen that other guy, the tent guy, before. In his tent in these woods at this very picnic table early in the morning. Seen him more than a few times.

Do I think that all black guys look alike? I want to believe I don't.

If not for this morning, would I have known that Tent Guy and Burger King are two entirely different black guys who might just share similar fashions and outside proclivities? In my head, I'd like to say yes, definitely, no question.

Have I walked my dogs past Tent Guy more than a few times and not said hello, not offered him a little cash to get a warm meal, not apologized when my dogs would bark and growl at him?

And here I am finally trying to pay my penance and ease my conscience and here is Burger King guy with his gold watch and retro Jordans.

I apologize again for trying to give him 20 bucks and he says nah, man, it ain't no thing. You just tryin to be a standup guy.

Yes. Yes, I am trying to be a standup guy.

It's always nice when black people are there to make uppity white peckerwoods like me feel better about us being ignorant uppity white peckerwoods.

Our fragile egos.

I say, Thanks, bro—I mean thanks *dude*.

I turn back to the car, the barking growling dogs. I take one last look at the Tent Guy passed out in his tent in the woods.

I finger the 20-dollar bill I've put back in my pocket.

And here I am again up in my head:

Do I go over and give him the money that I'd really meant to give him in the first place?

But also wake him up and maybe startle him, get him thinking that I was some asshole cop or librarian trying to kick him out of his tent in the woods again.

And risk making it all look performative to this other black guy, Mr. Burger King guy?

It's a quandary.

In some ways, that's the real problem with homelessness around here, when we finally see it and we're stuck telling ourselves we have to do something about it.

I'm still checking out Tent Guy for signs of life from a healthy distance as I get back in my car with the barking dogs—as I put the 20 bucks back in my wallet where I've hidden it under the seat, where nobody'd be tempted to steal the 20 bucks I've been trying to give away all morning.

Who do I imagine when I imagine somebody trying to steal my money? What does that person look like?

I'd like to tell you it would be some dirty meth-head Ted Kaczynski-looking white guy.

I'd like to tell you that's the first image that'd pop into mind.

Maybe some guy with mental illness. That's the real crisis, isn't it? The way we treat the mentally ill and the way we then think of them as threats to us simply because we didn't want to help them in the first place.

The way, really, we all deserve what we get in this life. The karma of homelessness. The karma of mental illness. The karma of institutional racism.

No, the real problem people don't think about— homelessness, mental illness, petty crime—it's not the 20 bucks they steal or even all the credit cards you have to cancel, or even the license you have to replace.

It's all the goddamn glass from breaking the window. It's the pain in the ass of not being able to park in certain easy-toaccess spots because you can't trust that your car won't get broken into again.

The guilt that comes along with all that. The faces you see when you look in the mirror, the rear-view mirror as you drive away as quickly as you can, the dark eyes looking back at you watching you go.

What are they thinking as they watch you go?

That's what I'm thinking about on my way home to go feed the dogs.

The special diet of wet food I'll mix in for the boykin lab. The pretty one with the discerning palate, the one that all the big old racist rednecks around town stop to compliment me on, whistle at, ask to pet, to stroke, to itch behind the ears.

Pull over in the middle of the road and roll down the windows of their shiny new F150s:

That there's a beaut of an huntin dog.

Bet she's bagged more than her share of birds in her life, ain't she, boss?

[*wolf-whistle*] Would'ya look at that baby girl right there. Ain't you a sweetheart, yes you are, yes you are. [*wolf-whistle*]

The one that everybody calls a *she*, even though he's a *he*—just a *he* with feathery soft chocolate caramel fur. Sinewy. *Bark bark growl bar*k—and nobody's afraid of *she's* gonna rip them limb from limb.

It's the mangy pitbull and the grizzly bear of a rottweiler having grown up on the streets. Abandoned by the same type of people who make you feel guilty when your dogs act like they're about to murder them.

Bark bark growl bark—they sadly just don't have the stomach for the fancy stuff.

Nope. Nothing but discount kibble for those two. Or I'll be cleaning up the diarrhea for days.

Gets so bad sometimes I'll have to leave them outside half the night to get it all out of their system. Lie there in bed with my boykin and break my heart listening to them howl and howl and whine and whine.

Wondering what it'd take for somebody to call the cops. The looks they'd give me when they see my two big ugly monsters out in the backyard. The questions of neglect or abuse or dog fighting.

All the questions I'd get if I didn't live in the neighborhood I live in and look like the middle-aged privilegedass peckerwood I've come to look like these days.

ACKNOWLEDGEMENTS

The following stories were previously published:
"Ray: Act I" in *HAD* (as Electrocution for Kids"),
"Ray: Act II" in *Expat Review* (as "Man's Search for Meaninglessness...")
"Boykin" in *Poverty House*
"Benjamin/Benjamin" in *Poverty House*
"Shonda" in The Laurel Review.

As always, for Ina. As always, I'm sorry.

For my family. As always, I'm sorry.

For AVW. As always, I'm sorry.

For Mike Chin, Tom Williams, Leland Cheuk, Sacha Bissonnette, and Alan Good: I'm sorry.

For Sam Pink whose work inspired a lot of this: I'm sorry.

For Sheldon Lee Compton, Aaron Burch, Manuel Marrero, and Luke Rolfes for publishing these stories originally and giving me the confidence to put together a whole collection: I'm sorry.

For the real-life people who inspired the very very loose portrayals of Boykin, Kelly, TC, Q, Jordan Benjamin, Kevin, Brian aka "Burger King Guy," and Clem, Mel, & Mikey: I'm sorry.

Made in the USA
Columbia, SC
10 September 2024